100+ IDEAS
FOR TEACHING LANGUAGES

CONTINUUM ONE HUNDREDS SERIES

100+ IDEAS
FOR TEACHING
LANGUAGES

Nia Griffith

BLOOMSBURY

LONDON · NEW DELHI · NEW YORK · SYDNEY

Published 2012 by Continuum
an imprint of Bloomsbury Publishing Plc
50 Bedford Square, London W1B 3DP

www.bloomsbury.com

ISBN: 978-0-8264-9763-5 (paperback)

© Nia Griffith 2007

First published 2005 by Continuum International Publishing Group
Reprinted 2009, 2011, 2012 (twice)

A CIP record for this publication is available from the British Library.

Typeset by Ben Cracknell Studios | www.benstudios.co.uk
Printed and bound in Great Britain

This book is produced using paper that is made from wood grown
in managed, sustainable forests. It is natural, renewable and
recyclable. The logging and manufacturing processes conform to
the environmental regulations of the country of origin.

CONTENTS

SECTION 2   Presenting or revising vocabulary

SECTION 3 Practising language structures

SECTION 4 Great games

SECTION 5 Active listening

SECTION 6 Creative writing

SECTION 8 **Extended project activities**

SECTION 9 **The more advanced pupil**

SECTION 10 **Involving native speakers**

APPENDIX

Ideas to use with many topics

PREPARATION

Many language teachers use picture cards (or flashcards) to practise the vocabulary that they want to present. Commercial courses often used to come with expensive flashcards, but many now provide pictures on CD which you can print out to make your own flashcards. It is important to make sure that the pictures are large enough to be seen clearly by the whole class.

This game can be played with any picture flashcards, such as those of food, clothes or furniture. You need at least nine flashcards and some Blu-Tack. Or you can use a pre-prepared overhead transparency (OHT).

ACTIVITY

Draw a noughts and crosses grid on the board (9 squares, 3 by 3). Make the squares in your grid big enough for your flashcards to fit, together with enough space for you to write a visible number in each. Number the squares 1 to 9 in the same corner of each square (for example top left). Introduce or revise the vocabulary by holding up each flashcard and then sticking it with Blu-Tack onto one square on the board. Continue until you have one picture stuck in each square on the board.

Then divide class into two teams and play noughts and crosses.

HOW TO PLAY NOUGHTS AND CROSSES

Turn to team A and ask a pupil to give the number of a square using the target language and say the correct word, for example 5, a cat. If the pupil answers correctly, put a small cross by the side of the picture. Then ask the same of a pupil from the opposing team and put a 0 by the picture for a correct answer. The winning team is the first team to make a line of three (horizontal, vertical or diagonal). If a pupil answers incorrectly, they do not get their 0 or X and the other team gets the chance to ask for their next choice of square. Pupils are much more motivated than when just responding to flashcards. You can use this activity simply for single words or you can demand a completely correct sentence which makes it much harder to win. You can be 'mean' by putting the most difficult words in the most useful squares, namely the centre square and the corners.

Chorusing is a very valuable way of giving pupils the practice they need in pronunciation and of drilling the language into them. Inevitably however some pupils may tend to daydream, so any techniques which help to keep pupils' attention and make the words or phrases more memorable are useful tools.

USING DIFFERENT VOICES

o using loud and soft voices;
o using different moods, for example an angry or sad mood;
o using different mannerisms, for example granddad, hippy, a celebrity, little child, disaffected teenager, angry parent or teacher, drunken football supporter.

ORCHESTRATING THE CLASS

o have one half of the class say the word, then the other half;
o say the words row by row or table by table;
o point to individual pupils or pairs of pupils to say the words;
o all the girls, all the boys.

MAKING CHORUSING FUN

You can use wildly exaggerated actions to keep pupils' attention. You may find that younger pupils will enjoy doing these actions with you but teenagers will probably just think you are eccentric. Never mind if it helps keep their attention and keeps them chorusing.

ANIMALS

Wiggle your hand vertically for a fish, dart your hand forward horizontally for a snake, do a rabbit's ears with your hands, stroke the cat, fill your cheeks out for a hamster, flap your arms for a bird, clip on the lead and walk the dog.

HOUSEHOLD TASKS

Zoom the vacuum cleaner/mop/brush vigorously around pupils' desks, wash and dry dishes, pretend to drop a plate, iron everything in sight, hold your nose as you take out the rubbish. A few props can help such as an empty box of washing powder or a washing-up liquid bottle.

MONTHS OF THE YEAR

As you chorus these in order, pupils have to put up their hands when you say the month in which they have a birthday. As a variation, the teacher can say the months in random order and the pupils who have a birthday in that month must put up their hands. You can get pupils to police each other and point out if a fellow pupil does not participate correctly.

GUESSING THE ACTION

One pupil does an action and the others have to guess what it is. The pupil who guesses correctly scores a point and does the next action (or they can pick the next pupil who has to do an action). Topics which work particularly well include sports, free-time activities, household tasks and daily routine. Pupils guessing can either practise the second person of the verb 'Are you playing tennis?' or the third person 'Is he/she playing tennis?' The person doing the action can just say yes/no or can be required to say the whole sentence 'Yes I am playing tennis' or 'No, I'm not playing tennis'.

Sources of songs can include:

1 children's nursery rhymes and action songs such as 'head, shoulders, knees and toes' that exist in the target language;
2 familiar songs from pupils' mother tongue of which you can write a target language version;
3 songs which already have versions in the target language and the pupils' mother tongue, for example 'Happy Birthday', Christmas carols such as 'Silent Night';
4 songs produced with coursebooks. These have the advantage of using the exact vocabulary that you want to teach but they vary somewhat in their singability!
5 songs currently in the target language charts that have appropriate language, even if you only do a few lines with pupils;
6 disco action songs that you can sing along to in the target language with the actions, such as 'Going to the Party' by Black Lace.

Point out to your cynical teenage classes that these songs are not necessarily the latest chart favourites of the target language country but rather songs that are useful to help them remember certain words.

USING SONGS AS LISTENING EXERCISES

Write out the words of a song but leave some gaps. The pupils can then listen to the song and write down the words that go in the gaps. You can target key items of vocabulary that they need to know or pick the second of two rhyming words. Where the song is very clearly linked to the vocabulary of the unit, you can actually stop the tape before the second of the rhyming words and see if any pupils can predict the word before you let them hear it.

Those of you who are super organized can have a song playing as pupils enter the classroom and settle down so that their brains are subconsciously tuning into the subject!

Remember that, although a lot of flashcards simply depict nouns, it is much more useful for pupils to have to practise phrases or whole sentences with them. For example, if using pictures of food, then pupils can be required to preface each noun with phrases such as 'I would like . . .', 'Have you any . . .?', 'I like/don't like . . .', 'I usually eat . . .'

Flashcards depicting verbs can be used to practise verbs in a range of tenses.

SAY THE WORD

Hold up the flashcards and pupils chorus the word, or pupils put up their hands and you ask one pupil to say the word.

TRUE/FALSE

If, for example, the teacher holds up a flashcard of a mouse and says 'It's a mouse', then pupils indicate 'true' by pointing their thumbs upwards. If the teacher says 'It's a cat', pupils indicate 'false' by pointing their thumbs downwards.

Speed up and play as a game, eliminating pupils who point their thumbs the wrong way or who are the slowest to react.

WHICH CARD?

This is a variation of the above in which the teacher holds one card out to the right and one card out to the left and says one of the words. Pupils then have to point to the correct card. If the teacher says a word which is on neither card, then pupils must keep their hands by their sides. Add pace by picking up different cards and by swapping cards from one hand to the other.

POINT TO THE CARD

As you teach/revise the cards, pin them up around the room so that they will be visible to pupils when they are standing up. Pupils all stand up and have to point to the correct card, according to which word the teacher says. Eliminate pupils who point to the wrong card or who are the slowest to get there. Pupils sit down when they are eliminated so that it is easy to see who is still in.

GUESS WHICH CARD

Shuffle the cards and carefully select one card and put it somewhere safe (e.g. face down on the table) without letting anyone see which one it is. Pupils have to guess the card and the pupil who guesses correctly can then come out and hide another card.

HIDE THE CARD

Send one pupil out of the room and hide a flashcard. When the pupil comes back into the room, the class has to chorus the word on the flashcard repeatedly, getting louder as the pupil approaches the flashcard and getting quieter as the pupil moves away from the card until the pupil finds it.

HOLD UP THE CARD

Use three or four sets of the same flashcards (for example four sets of seven animals for a class of 28). Give one card to each pupil and, when you say a word, all the pupils who have that card must hold up their card. Award a point for the first pupil to raise their hand.

These ideas are suitable for using with small items that can easily be brought into the classroom, such as classroom objects, cutlery and crockery, toilet articles such as toothpaste or soap, food packets, real fruit and vegetables, clothes and, if you have access to children's small toys, then you can use all manner of amazing things these days, from vehicles (car, lorry, fire engine) to dolls' house furniture. Just make sure that the object is big enough to see.

Most of the flashcard activities can also be used with small objects. In addition, the following can add variety.

WHAT'S IN THE BAG/ENVELOPE?

Put a number of objects into a bag or a large envelope before pupils arrive for the lesson. Introduce or recap the vocabulary using other means such as an OHT or a textbook. Then ask the pupils to guess what is in the bag. Each time a pupil makes a correct guess, take the appropriate item out of the bag and show it to the pupils.

WHAT'S IN THE BAGS/ENVELOPES?

As above but one put item in each bag/envelope. For added novelty, you can let pupils feel the bag before they guess.

GUESS WHICH ITEM

If you want pupils to play this game with objects instead of cards (see Idea 6) use a very large cardboard box (which pupils cannot see into) in which you keep all the objects. Then put a bag into the box and slide one object into it, to be the hidden object.

PASS ME THE SALT PLEASE

Point to a pupil who has to ask for one of the objects, by saying a phrase such as 'Pass me the bread please'. Continue asking a different pupil each time until all the objects have been given out. Then ask a pupil who is not holding any object to ask for an object. The pupil who is holding the object requested has to bring it over. There is no scoring or winning in this activity but it is appropriate for teaching phrases such as 'please may I have a . . .' and it works particularly well if there is something about the item that makes the pupils want to see it more closely (for example a mug with a cartoon character on it).

Divide pupils up into groups, for example seven groups of four. Make sure that the groups are a fairly even distance away from you. This means that you may need to stand in the middle of the classroom and/or rearrange some classroom furniture.

Ask the pupils to number the members of their group (1, 2, 3, 4). If you have a group of only three, then one person will need to double up and be number one and number four. More than four pupils in a group tends to mean that some pupils do not participate very effectively.

The aim of the game is that one member of each group brings you, the teacher, the items that you request. So for example, you say 'Bring me a pen, number three' and then pupil number three in each group has to bring you a pen. You can award one point to each group that brings you the correct item, and two points to the group that is the first to get the item to you.

To extend this beyond classroom objects, if pupils have a textbook, you can ask for 'a picture of . . .' and pupils have to bring you the book open at a suitable picture.

BRING ME

Games can include:

1 chorus numbers forwards;
2 chorus numbers backwards;
3 count around the class – point to pupils who, in turn, have to say the next number;
4 count around the class in intervals of two (2, 4, 6, 8), five (5, 10, 15, 20), ten (10, 20, 30), etc.;
5 count around the class but change direction every so often.

FINGER NUMBERS

When you say a number, pupils have to put up that number of fingers. Can be used for numbers 1–10 or can be adapted for 10, 20, 30. Play as a game, starting with pupils standing up and making them sit down when they are eliminated, after holding up the wrong number of fingers or being the slowest to get there.

FIZZ BUZZ FOR BUDDING MATHEMATICIANS

Count around the class but every time you get to a number that is divisible by three, the pupil must say 'fizz' instead of the number, and every time a number is divisible by five they must say 'buzz'. For a number like 15 which is divisible both by three and five, they must say 'fizz buzz'. So the game might start like this: one, two, fizz, four, buzz, fizz, seven, eight, fizz buzz.

This can be used not just for numbers but for any defined list of vocabulary, and can be a useful filler if you have a couple of minutes left at the end of a lesson.

QUICK NUMBER BINGO

At its simplest, ask pupils to write down in figures any three numbers within a specified range (for example three numbers between 60 and 80) and get the person sitting next to them to check which numbers they have written down so that they do not change them part way through the game. When you say the numbers in that range, pupils must cross out the ones they have and the first to cross all their numbers out and shout bingo (or preferably the target language equivalent) and is the winner.

A LONGER VERSION

Can consist of a grid of 9 squares, 3 by 3, and the first pupil to get a line vertically, horizontally or diagonally shouts bingo and is the first winner. You can then go on until a pupil has a complete 'house', i.e. all nine numbers crossed out. You can also make a rectangle, 4 × 3, but then you need to clarify what you mean by a diagonal line, if you allow one at all.

USING VOCABULARY OTHER THAN NUMBERS

This game can also be used for any clearly specified vocabulary list, for example, draw pictures/write the words for any three of the subjects to be learnt that day. This is a useful way of recapping the lesson.

MAKING CARDS

Give each pupil a card on which they have to draw a nine-square grid and draw a picture in each square. Make sure that pupils have a closed list of the vocabulary they can choose from (e.g. a list of animals, furniture). You can actually make a series of cards yourself quite quickly on a computer, making each one just a bit different from the last one, by moving pictures about. To be able to reuse these cards, you will not want pupils to write on them so think what you will use as counters to cover the squares that have been called. One way is to give pupils a piece of scrap paper and let them tear off a bit of paper each time they need a counter.

11

A CLOCK EACH

This is time-consuming the first time but it is well worth it if you keep the clocks you make and use them again and again with different classes. The activity encourages every pupil in the class to concentrate, rather than day-dreaming and leaving a few pupils to answer all the questions. Pupils enjoy the novelty of handling the clocks and they can be used as a five-minute revision activity at any time.

Make a cardboard clock for each pupil by cutting out a circle of card, for example the largest circle that you can fit onto an A4 piece of card. Write the numbers of the clock in thick felt-tip pen, making them as large as you can. You may wish to include the 24-hour clock times underneath the 12-hour clock. I prefer not to, putting up support for the 24-hour clock on the board when it is needed (for example 13 = 1, 14 = 2). Make the hands out of a different colour card and fix them to the centre of the clock using a paper fastener.

Give each pupil a clock and ask them to place it face up on the table. When you say the time, pupils have to move the hands of the clock to the correct time. It is advisable to keep the minute hand (the long hand) still to start with, for example pointing to the 12 and just require pupils to move the hour hand, by saying times such as 6pm, 8pm, 9pm. Then do times such as 4.30pm, 7.30pm, 10.30pm then 3.15am, 5.15am, etc. Then you can do times in which the pupils keep the hour hand still and move the minute hand. When pupils are thoroughly familiar with the 12-hour clock, you can introduce the 24-hour clock. Pupils often find this very difficult and you may decide to put up number support on the board as mentioned above.

Although it can take a little while to teach pupils how to play this game, it is an excellent way of motivating pupils to speak. Once you have taught pupils how to play the game with one set of cards, you will find that you can easily repeat the same game with them, using different sets of cards. Be very clear about what language you want pupils to practise – see topic ideas below.

I used to think that you should not give pupils too much linguistic help on the cards but, in fact, if you do not provide some words on the cards, you are effectively only practising what pupils already know. If, however, you write the appropriate phrases/sentences on the cards, they can actually be used to reinforce language that the pupils have only just met. This way they hear and say the same phrases over and over again, so that they know them much better by the end of the game. For this use, I find that writing the words they need to say on the cards works well.

INSTRUCTIONS

The object of the game is to collect sets of four of the same card or belonging to the same family. The player who collects the most sets of cards by the end of the game is the winner. (If you operate a reward system, you can award a point for each set of four cards so that most pupils will get something.)

1 Three or four players required.
2 Shuffle and deal out five cards to each player.
3 Put the remainder of the cards in a pile face down in the centre.
4 The first player (Fred) decides which set of cards he wants to collect (you can only ask for a card if you have one of that set in your hand). Fred then chooses one of the other players and asks him/her if he/she has that card, e.g.:
   'John, have you got a rabbit?'
5 If John has any rabbits, he must hand them *all* over and then Fred can ask again, either asking another player or asking John for a different card.
   If John has not got any rabbits, then Fred picks up the top card from the pile on the table and it is the next person's go.
6 If a person runs out of cards, they can take the top card from the pile on the table to carry on.

13

MAKING THE SETS OF CARDS

Sets of 32 cards, that is eight sets of four, are easy to create and make the game last a reasonable amount of time. To make, divide a sheet of A4 into eight little rectangles and draw/paste a different picture into each one. Photocopy onto card. You will need to make four copies of this for each set of cards you want, so, if you want nine sets of cards, you will need 36 copies.

SOME TOPICS THAT CAN BE EXPLOITED WITH THE HAPPY FAMILIES/FISH CARD GAME

1 Familiar questions, for example 'Have you got . . .?', and pets.
2 Formal questions such as shopping, 'Have you got . . .?', and food, clothes, souvenirs, lost property items. Equally 'I would like . . .'
3 Better motivated pupils who can manipulate language can use this game for practising verbs:
Pupil A: 'Do you play tennis?'
Pupil B: 'Yes, I do play tennis.' or 'No, I don't play tennis.'
4 Role-play or letter-writing language can also be practised. One set of cards I made had an appropriate picture and one of the sentences below on each card and I have found it to be one of the few successful ways of getting lower-ability pupils to practise role-play sentences repeatedly. Likewise, with other topics such as campsite, train tickets, etc.

a I'd like a single room.
b I'd like a room with a shower.
c I'd like a room with a bath.
d I'd like a hotel with a swimming pool.
f I'd like to pay a maximum of . . .
g I'd like breakfast included.
h I'd like to stay for three nights.

One of the advantages of the overhead projector (OHP) is that you can make the overhead transparencies (OHTs) using the best pictures that you can find. One way in which the overhead projector is particularly flexible is the fact that you can place one OHT over another. This means that you can make one OHT with pictures representing the vocabulary that you want to teach. If you then place this OHT on the OHP and place a blank OHT on top of it, you can make what we call an overlay. On the overlay you might choose, for example, to write the vocabulary that goes with the pictures. You would then have what we could call a 'base' OHT with pictures on it and an overlay with vocabulary. You can then present the language by using the base OHT and the overlay together, so that pupils can see the pictures and the vocabulary. Then, as pupils become more confident about the language, remove the overlay with the vocabulary and drill the language using the picture overlay without the written support. You can make several overlays for the same set of pictures, for example past/present/future versions for verb pictures or weather symbols.

USE OF OVERLAYS AS ANSWER SHEETS

On your base sheet write the exercise, for example, a gap-filling exercise or a multiple choice question and then make an overlay with the answers on, preferably in a different colour.

CREATING MOVEMENT ON THE OHP

For example, a bus or train arriving/departing. You can use bits of OHT acetate with a long strip of acetate attached to them. For example a picture of a train or bus could have a long strip attached to the front of it and as you pull the strip, holding your hand off the OHP, the train or bus moves along. Make a base OHT with a railway platform or bus stop to practise arriving/departing.

USING OVERLAYS

You can make mini acetates by using small bits of acetate, each with one picture on it. You can often make these by photocopying a pageful of pictures onto acetate and cutting it up.

Ways of using mini acetates

1   Use as though they are flashcards by placing one small bit of acetate with a picture on it on the OHP at a time. You can then adapt many of the flashcard ideas for use with these mini acetates.

2   Place several of these mini acetates on the OHP and practise the vocabulary with pupils. Then cover the OHP with a sheet of paper to remove one of the mini acetates. Pupils have to guess which picture is missing.

3   Younger pupils enjoy coming out to put a mini acetate on the correct place on the OHP according to your instructions, for example on a base OHT showing first, second, third road to the left/right they can place small pictures of buildings when you say for example 'The church is in the third road on the left' or 'To get to the church, take the third road on the left.' Other pupils in the class can volunteer instructions and, as the pieces are movable, there is plenty of scope for repetition and variety. As a follow-up activity, pupils can draw a similar diagram in response to written or spoken instructions and you can use the OHP for them to check their answers.

Using football is a good way of motivating pupils, especially boys. It is even better if you can relate what you are doing to recent or imminent events. If you are not much of a fan yourself, then get colleagues or older pupils to help you.

1   At the simplest level, practise numbers by reading out football scores.
2   Nationalities: make a quiz with clues such as the following:
    A Frenchman who plays for Arsenal
    Make sure you know what the answers are and if there are alternative answers. Don't forget to update the quiz if you use it again later on. When you use it in class, be aware that some pupils may not know much about football, but they may be happy to interpret the sentence and then others guess the answer.
3   Use colour pictures of footballers in their team colours to practise colours.
4   Use international events like the World Cup to practise the names of countries.
5   Use fixtures lists for the coming weekend to practise predictions: 'I think that X will beat Y.'
6   Use well-known players for any of the activities in this book involving celebrities, such as the quiz on family members.

USING TEENAGE MAGAZINES

SELECTING AND ORGANIZING YOUR MATERIALS

You will need quite a lot of time to prepare these exercises and many items will have a limited shelf life as the thrill of using such materials for pupils is the fact that they are relevant and up-to-date. Share work as much as possible with colleagues who have parallel classes.

CLASS SET OF MAGAZINES

Buying enough copies of a foreign language magazine to be shared one between two pupils can be expensive, but pupils really enjoy actually handling the magazines. It also means all pupils can work through the same exercises at the same time. It can take some organization when you are purchasing the magazines. After choosing a magazine that will offer you the best possibilities for exploitation, you will probably need to go around to several shops and count the number of copies available in each shop before you buy them, as, if there are not enough copies of your first choice available in the local area, you may have to buy a different magazine!

USE A MINI-LIBRARY OF DIFFERENT MAGAZINES

You can buy different magazines, again with enough copies overall for the whole class, but different pupils will be working on different magazines. This means that you can cater for different interest groups by using magazines such as football magazines and music magazines. Pupils still have the joy of handling them but you will have to prepare different exercises for the different magazines.

PAGES CUT OUT OF ONE MAGAZINE

This means that you only need to purchase one or two magazines. You can cut out a number of pages and put these into separate polypockets together with a worksheet with questions about the page. Make sure that each one is numbered so that pupils can keep a record of which pages they have done. You always need more pages than the number of pupils, to allow for the fact that some pupils finish sooner than others. This requires a lot of initial preparation but you then have a number of different exercises that pupils can work through.

PHOTOCOPIES OF ONE PAGE

This is the simplest for preparation and classroom management and can be a good way of finding out how well the activity works. The disadvantage is that the photocopies do not have the same appeal as the magazine itself.

Reading and understanding articles in the target language is very important in helping to build up pupils' vocabulary and their ability to cope with the unknown. This is a frequent component of examinations. Pupils can be encouraged simply to read for gist or for a much more detailed understanding of the language. While many textbooks provide reading comprehension exercises, the advantage of using target language magazines is that the materials you choose can be of particular interest or relevance to your pupils. The disadvantage is that you have to write the comprehension exercises yourself! Below you will find some ideas you can use to vary the type of exercises that you write.

WHICH PAGES TO USE?

Short articles on new film or music releases, or on details of celebrities' personal lives are often of interest to pupils, but all sorts of things can be exploited, even the advertisements.

TYPES OF QUESTION THAT CAN BE USED

1 Questions in the mother tongue – this can be particularly useful when the articles are a bit difficult for pupils and you need to provide some help through the question.
2 Questions in the target language.
3 True/false statements in the target language or mother tongue.
4 Multiple-choice questions.
5 Table to fill in, perhaps with personal and professional details for someone famous, for example favourite colour, films made.
6 A summary (or sentences) about the article with gaps in it. For less advanced pupils, provide a list of words that can go into the gaps.
7 Who says? This is particularly appropriate where a number of people are giving their opinion on an issue.
8 Writing a summary of the news item or article in the target language or in their mother tongue.

9 Rewriting as full sentences information which has been given in note form, such as a portrait of a star giving details such as age and place of birth.

10 Matching two halves of a sentence to reflect the sense of the article, for example:

He was born in . . . New York.

His mother was . . . a cleaner.

You can put in more second halves of the sentence than you actually need as distractors.

11 Match a theme/word/sentence to a paragraph of the text.

12 Find a word in the text with the same meaning/the opposite meaning.

—D ça va (Mary glasgow magazine).

get copies

There are three main forms of display material that are appropriate for the language classroom, namely linguistic prompts, pupils' work and cultural items appropriate to the target language. Consult primary-trained colleagues, classroom support assistants or your art department for extra advice about how to enhance your displays.

LINGUISTIC PROMPTS

Can include permanent displays such as classroom language, days of the week, months of the year, numbers, colours, and temporary displays of the vocabulary relevant to the unit that you are doing. Remember that you can pin a piece of paper on the wall and use the OHP to project a large version of a picture you may want to use.

PUPILS' WORK

Might include identity cards or introductory penfriend letters (with a photo if consent is given), decorated menus, price lists using topic vocabulary, posters for events, bar graphs or pie charts produced using the results of class surveys and clothes cut out from fashion magazines or sports magazines and labelled. For events like the world cup, football kit can be labelled with colours and the name of the country in the target language.

CULTURAL ITEMS

Might include maps, celebrity posters, tourist posters and posters advertising events.

Presenting or revising vocabulary

STAFF JACKETS

This activity adds interest to learning/revising vocabulary for clothes or lost property and can include materials (leather, wool, etc.) and colours.

PREPARATION

Arrange with colleagues to borrow various items that pupils will associate readily with them (e.g. leather jacket, suit jacket). The easiest items are coats, but you may find other items that are characteristic of members of staff such as bags, scarves, etc. Pupils are much more interested in saying 'It's Mrs Brown's shoe' than responding to a flashcard.

ACTIVITY

Hold up the items to practise the vocabulary first: 'It is a red coat', and then go through the items again asking pupils to guess whose coat it is. This can either be done as class oral work or you can ask each pupil to write down a sentence for each item as you hold it up.

Don't forget to return everything promptly at the end.

PREPARATION

You need as many C4 envelopes as there are pairs or groups of pupils and a few to spare. Into each envelope put one A4-sized piece of card onto which you have stuck a picture that you have taken out of a magazine. You will find that you can exploit the language better if the picture shows more than one person. They can simply be pictures of fashion models but pupils will find them more interesting if they are pictures of celebrities. In the envelope, together with the picture, place about 10 strips of card, on each one of which you have written a sentence such as 'He is wearing a black tie', 'She is wearing a green skirt'. Most of the sentences should be true statements about the picture, but also include a few distractors. There does not need to be the same number of true statements and distractors in each envelope. Make sure that you devise a labelling system so that if you drop a statement card, you know which envelope it belongs in, for example write a letter A on the back of everything that belongs in envelope A. It is best to write these statements on the computer as there is so much repetition in them. Print out, photocopy onto card and guillotine.

THE ACTIVITY

Pupils work in pairs or groups. Give each pair an envelope and ask them to place the correct statements on the picture and put the remainder away in the envelope. Walk around checking pupils' work. When they have finished one, they can put all the pieces away in the envelope and swap envelopes with another pair. Continue until pupils seem confident about the vocabulary involved. You can ask pupils to read out the sentences they have chosen. Follow-up work can include copying the statements into their books or pupils finding their own pictures and writing sentences about them.

HALF-EATEN FOOD IN A LUNCHBOX

Use this to practise phrases and vocabulary associated with food and to introduce or revise the past tense.

PREPARATION

Collect together various items of half-eaten food such as a banana skin, apple core, orange peel, half-eaten sandwich, empty crisp packet. Pupils always love the disgusting! If you want to keep smells to a minimum, or if you intend to ask pupils to hold them up, then wrap them in clingfilm or put them in small plastic bags. Then put all the items into one lunchbox or into several boxes. If using several boxes, you can repeat some of the vocabulary.

ACTIVITY

Decide which person of the verb you want pupils to practise (I, you, he, etc.) and demonstrate using one lunchbox, for example 'For my lunch I ate . . .' Then pick volunteer pupils and let them open the successive lunchboxes and say the appropriate sentences.

With so much concern about what we are eating these days, you can make your contribution by encouraging pupils to think about what they eat. Instead of just learning the words for food and drink, pupils can categorize items according to how healthy they are. There are various ways in which you can do this.

RED/AMBER/GREEN ON THE BOARD

Draw three columns on the board – red, amber, green – and explain to pupils that red is for fattening foods that we should reconsider eating, green is for foods that we can eat as much of as we like and amber is in between. After you have held up each food/drink flashcard and practised the vocabulary, ask pupils to say where each one should be put. Then fix the card to the appropriate column on the board using Blu-Tack.

USING SMALL CARDS IN PAIRS/GROUPS

Give each pair/group a set of small cards with the names of food items on them. Include in each set three cards with the headings red, amber and green. Pupils must lay out these headings and place the foods under the correct one. Alternatively, if you have coloured sheets of paper, you could give each pair a piece of red, amber and green paper on which they place the food cards. As follow-up work, pupils can write this up in their books, either as simple columns and lists of words or using sentences such as 'In the red column you find/we put . . . '

DISPLAY WORK

Make red, amber and green sections on the wall and ask pupils to produce pictures or magazine cuttings which they have labelled in the target language and pin these up in the correct section on the wall.

You can use this activity to teach the past tense and food (or any other item – whales can swallow anything, including luxury yachts and their contents!).

Cut a fat whale shape out of card and place it on the OHT and slide underneath it small OHT transparency pictures (mini acetates) of food and also include a surprise item such as a boy.

Start by asking the class what they think the whale had for breakfast. Make discreet coughing noises or disgusting sick noises and carefully drag out each item from under the whale so pulling them out of the whale's mouth and say 'For lunch I ate . . .'

When you have been through all the items once, put all the items back underneath the whale and repeat, revealing items slowly with pupils trying to guess them before they are fully coughed up and saying the sentences: 'For lunch I ate . . .'

THE DUSTBIN

A similar activity can be done with a cardboard dustbin and dustbin lid. Place the small acetate pictures under the dustbin, lift open the lid and pull them out of the bin one by one. You could also have a cat standing proudly by the bin, saying what he ate.

Use theme tunes of well-known programmes and have pupils guess what type of programme it is: 'It's a soap', 'It's a sports programme', etc. If you're very talented, sing them! If not, record them. (One can often get recordings – ask around, particularly if any colleagues are involved with local pub quizzes.)

Initially you may need to play quite a lot of the tune for pupils to recognize it, but you can then do follow-up work where you fast-forward the tape and randomly pick a bit for them to listen to. Play just a tiny extract and see if anyone can get the answer. Play more if necessary or to ascertain whether the guess was correct or not.

You can also use these theme tunes to practise opinions: 'I think X is great', or practise verb tenses, for example present: 'Do you watch X?', past 'Did you watch . . .?' and future 'Are you going to watch . . .?'

THEME TUNES

PREPARATION

On an OHT write about five questions for round one, asking who is whose relation, for example 'Who is Ralf Schumacher's brother?' Prepare about four OHTs in all for four rounds. Try to make sure that your rounds cover different interest groups and that there are a fair number of questions that most pupils will know. You might have one round on sport, one on TV soaps, one on music personalities and one on film stars, and obviously include all the family relative words that you want to practise, particularly those that are not so well remembered by teenage classes such as wife, husband, son, daughter, grandchild.

PUPILS WORK IN PAIRS OR TEAMS

Display the first round of questions on the OHT and read out the questions and allow pupils a reasonable amount of time to write down the answers. Advise pupils that if they do not know the answer immediately, they should jot down the question so that they can return to it later. Then whisk away the OHT for round one and display the OHT for round two. After the final round, allow pupils a minute or two to fill in any gaps. At the end, pupils can swap their answers with a neighbouring team to be marked as you go through the answers. Exploit the language to the maximum as you go through the answers, re-reading each question and making the pupils say a full-sentence reply.

WRITTEN FOLLOW-UP IN CLASS OR AT HOME

Pupils each write five similar-style questions (and supply the answers to them). You then take them in and use the most appropriate questions to produce a quiz for next time. Alternatively, you can ask pupils to write each question, with the answer in brackets, on a small piece of paper which you fold up and put in a hat. You then do the quiz by pulling out a question and reading it aloud.

This activity can be used to teach lost property vocabulary, such as keys, wallet, sunglasses, passport, mobile, or clothes or toilet articles and how to say X's bag. You can also include rooms of the house because celebrities' hotel bedrooms can often be mini-apartments that consist of rooms such as kitchen, lounge, bathroom, bedroom, balcony, etc. You can use simply 'was'/'is' or 'we have found', or the passive.

PREPARATION

Prepare a few visual props to help – background picture of hotel on screen/OHP, divided into floors and rooms and showing which celebrity is in which room, either just by writing up names or by using magazine pictures of stars which you pin on the board. You then need some lost-property items or magazine pictures of these items, such as footballer's shorts of the right team colour, expensive-looking sunglasses, etc.

ACTIVITY

Introduce your hotel plan and the celebrities who are occupying the rooms.

Then, to start with, you can hold up the items/magazine pictures of items and ask pupils to suggest who they belong to, by asking questions such as 'Whose football shirt is this?' and getting pupils to say 'It's X's football shirt.' Drill all the items a few times and then you can move on to sentences such as 'We've found X's wallet in Y's bedroom' – obviously include any recent scandals or pair up likely/unlikely couples!

Ask pupils to make similar sentences by asking 'Where have we found X's dress?' Pupils enjoy saying or writing their own sentences.

A number of commercial courses provide copymasters from which you can make small sets of cards, which often consist of picture cards and word cards. With the wealth of visual material now available on the Internet, you can also make your own sets of cards. These can be used in a number of ways such as a starter activity to revise work or as a quick break from teacher presentation to check how much pupils have taken in. If pupils work in pairs, this means making fewer sets of cards and is also more fun. It is well worth putting a distinguishing mark on the back of each card, such as an A on all the cards in one set, a B on the next set, etc. so that if a card drops onto the floor you can put it back with the correct set.

MATCHING UP CARDS

Pupils place the cards face up and match the words and pictures. This can be done as a race with the first pair to finish putting up their hands.

PELMANISM OR PAIRS

Pupils shuffle the cards and place them face downwards on the table. Pupil A turns over two cards. If they make a pair, pupil A keeps them and has another go. If they do not make a pair, pupil A turns them face downwards again and it is pupil B's turn.

DISTRACTORS

You can make sets of cards which include distractors so that for eight picture cards you might have a choice of 12 words. This requires pupils to do a bit more reading and thinking. The distractors can require pupils to look carefully at detail, for example to choose between 'I play tennis when the sun shines' and 'I play tennis when it rains'.

BEGINNINGS AND ENDINGS

As a change from finding pairs of identical cards, you can also make sets of cards in which pupils have to match up pairs of cards, one with the beginning of a sentence and one with the end of a sentence.

OPPOSITES ATTRACT

You can make sets of cards with pairs of opposites, for example hot/cold, fat/thin, big/small.

PICTURE AND SENTENCE

Another variation is for pupils to match a picture card to a card with a sentence.

CHECK YOUR GRAMMAR

More demanding games can be devised by making sets of cards with pairs which depend on grammatical accuracy (e.g. adjectives or verbs which need to agree).

QUESTION AND ANSWER

Make sets of cards in which the pairs consist of a question and an answer. When pupils have matched up all the pairs of cards, they can read them out as a dialogue, with one pupil reading the questions and the other reading the answers. They can then practise them again, adapting the answer to express their own circumstances/viewpoint. For example:

Q: Where do you live?
A: I live in . . .
Q: What sort of music do you like?
A: I like . . .

MORE IDEAS FOR PAIRS/PELMANISM

'Who Wants to be a Millionaire?' has versions in many different languages. It is possible to download the format, including the music, from the Internet and into PowerPoint and, if you have a data projector, you can then project it for everyone to see. To find out which countries have the programme visit the Who Wants to be a Millionaire website at http://millionaire.itv.com/millionaire/home.php. You can create textboxes at the bottom of the screen onto which you type questions. It is then very easy to edit the questions to make different versions of the quiz for different topics. It is ideal if you can get the target-language version with their title and presenter, but if not use your own country's.

If you do not have a data projector available, then you can make an overhead transparency of the introduction to the programme to create the atmosphere and capture pupils' interest and then use questions written on overhead transparencies. You can then say each question in the slow and deliberate way that they do on the programme and this can give you a chance to make pupils listen repeatedly to the particular structures and vocabulary that you choose to use.

WRITTEN ANSWERS

Instead of playing as a quiz between teams or groups, you can also ask all pupils to write down the answers which can help to focus their attention better. Pupils can also get more practice in writing questions if they have to write some questions and suggested answers. You can then choose the best questions to put in your next quiz.

The topic of household chores is most unappealing, particularly to teenage boys, who are certainly not going to admit to doing any (you can get in lots of practice of 'Nothing' and 'Never'!), so introduce it with various robots which have their own specific tasks. To practise the first person of the verb, use a speech bubble in which the robot says what it does. Give each robot an appropriate name, such as Rose for the gardening robot. Prepare an OHT or worksheet with several robots, such as those below. Present to the class and do comprehension and repetition work. Written follow-up: draw a robot and say what it does.

Cordon bleu:
I do the cooking
I lay the table
I clear the table
I do the washing-up
I tidy the plates

Rally:
I do the shopping
I do the housework
I do the cooking
I clean the bathroom
I lay the table

Rose:
I do the gardening
I sweep the garage
I walk the dog
I take out the rubbish

Miracle:
I do the hoovering
I clean the bathroom
I tidy the bedrooms
I make the beds

ELEPHANTS DRINKING WINE

1 Draw an elephant on the board with its trunk hovering above a full glass of wine as if it is about to drink, and practise the sentence 'I am about to drink the wine' (or 'He/it is about to drink . . .').

2 Then elongate the trunk into the glass and rub out some of the wine to practise the sentence 'I am in the middle of drinking the wine.'

3 Finally, rub out the rest of wine and practise the sentence 'I have just drunk/he has just drunk the wine.'

CHOCOLATES ON A TRAY

As a follow-up treat at the end of the lesson, present a tray of chocolates/sweets, but before each pupil is allowed to take one, he/she has to say 'I am about to eat a chocolate.' You can then insist that they say 'I have just eaten a chocolate' before they pack away.

This idea can be used to teach or revise spare-time activities and to revise various persons of verbs in the past and present and words for saying how often (everyday, rarely, or using days of the week). I find it particularly useful for practising the we/they forms of the verb. You can also use it for daily routine or lifestyle activities such as smokes, drinks, eats too much.

Draw bizarre alien creatures on an OHT or worksheet (e.g., square screen-shaped bodies for the planet where they watch too much television/long-limbed creatures for the sporty planet/beer bellies for the drinkers). Make their names and/or the names of their planets link in to their activities. Give them a speech bubble saying 'I . . .' or shared speech bubble saying 'We . . .' Drill the verbs/activities using different persons of the verb as appropriate. Follow-up work can include pupils producing their own creatures, together with speech bubbles.

BEFORE/AFTER SCENARIO AND NEW YEAR'S RESOLUTIONS

Create a 'before' and 'after' version of the unhealthy creatures to practise the habitual past 'We used to . . .' and contrast it with the present 'Now we . . .'

Likewise the unhealthy creatures can make New Year's resolutions and you can draw the slimmed-down versions in dream bubbles.

EXAMPLE CREATURES

Square slugs:
We watch TV
We play computer games
We listen to music

Sporty snakes:
We play football
We play tennis
We go swimming

Brainy bats:
We read books
We do our homework
We speak lots of languages

Bloated blobs:
We eat, we drink
We eat, we drink
We eat, we drink

CREATURES FROM DIFFERENT PLANETS

IDEA
34

VOLCANO – WHAT WERE YOU DOING WHEN . . . ?

USE OF APPROPRIATE PAST TENSES
These suggestions are for scenarios to help practise the different past tenses.

PREPARATION
If you have any appropriate pictures of things such as volcanoes erupting, then use these. Similarly you could set the scene with pictures of the ruins of Pompeii, which was swamped in the lava from a volcano in AD 79. You can use up-to-date events as long as you are aware of any personal sensitivities pupils may have. You also need to have ready the difficult vocabulary/phrases that will be needed.

ACTIVITY
First practise saying 'I was in . . .' with, for example, places around the town or rooms in the house.

Then ask the question 'Where were you at the time the volcano erupted?' and practise sentences such as 'I was in the kitchen at the time the volcano erupted.'

Follow with sentences such as 'I was eating', 'I was sleeping.'

Then ask the question of another pupil, 'What were you doing when the volcano erupted?'

Another response might be 'I was watching television when the volcano erupted.'

OTHER EVENTS
When the earthquake happened
When the bomb exploded
When X scored the winning goal

This is another activity which practises the use of appropriate past tenses.

PREPARATION

Prepare a brief scenario of a crime, saying simply 'There has been a murder in an airport', or 'There has been a robbery in a department store', but don't give any details.

Place in an envelope the details of where *exactly* the crime took place.

ACTIVITY

Practise the vocabulary you will need, such as the places around the airport (information desk, newsagent, check-in, duty-free, cafeteria, lift, Gate no. 4, etc.), or the departments in the department store.

Practise asking 'Where were you at the time of the crime?' Pupils have to respond by saying 'I was in . . . at the time of the crime.'

Then ask again 'What were you doing at the time of the crime?', to which pupils have to respond differently with sentences such as 'I was buying a newspaper.'

Ask each pupil to write down about four sentences saying where they were and what they were doing. Tell them that they have to make their story sound as convincing as possible. More advanced pupils can mention an alibi and use third-person verbs, for example 'I was with my friend who was buying a drink.' Then you can act as the detective by interviewing pupils, asking them to read out their sentences.

You can either interview all pupils or pick pupils randomly, or you can state a characteristic that will eliminate some pupils. When you've finished, open the envelope with the details the crime. If there is only one pupil who has mentioned that place, he/she is automatically the criminal. If there is more than one pupil, then all the pupils who mentioned that place have to come out to the front. You then interview these pupils again and the class has to decide which one has the least convincing story and is therefore the criminal.

AT THE TIME OF THE CRIME I WAS . . . .

If you are worried that no pupil will mention the place in the envelope, you can cheat by preparing several envelopes in your bag, although you tell the pupils there's only one. Just make sure you have a way of pulling the correct envelope out of your bag!

This activity helps to practise the appropriate past tense.

PREPARATION

Bring in some old children's things from your past. The more pupils can laugh at them the better. They might include a vinyl record, old comic/annual, or clothes. Don't forget you'll probably be using some things that pupils would consider old-fashioned! If you have thrown everything away, then look on the internet for things such as old pictures of pop stars, old cars or old football players.

ACTIVITY

Present the items to the pupils, saying sentences such as 'When I was young, I used to read . . ., I used to listen to . . ., I used to love . . ., I used to follow . . . (football team), we used to have. . . (old car), I used to collect. . .'

Then encourage pupils to produce similar sentences in response to questions such as 'When you were little, what did you used to watch on television?', 'What school did you used to go to?', 'Where did you used to live?'

Pupils can follow this up with written work on what they used to do.

GHOSTS

To add variety, you can sketch a quick picture of a castle wall with two ghosts peering over the top. You can give each ghost a speech bubble in which he/she is saying 'When I was young, I used to . . .' After practising appropriate language pupils can then write a dialogue between the ghosts discussing what they used to when they were young. More advanced pupils could describe what life was like when the ghosts were young.

It can be very difficult to draw convincing pictures of people with various occupations so this activity uses the items that various professionals would use.

PREPARATION

Collect together a number of items that could be considered typical of particular professions – usually either a tool they use or an item they make, for example letters (postman/woman), scissors and comb (hairdresser), loaf of bread (baker), spanner (mechanic), builder's trowel (builder), plane (a carpenter), markbook (teacher), thermometer (nurse/doctor), microphone (singer), football (footballer).

ACTIVITY

Use the items to practise jobs in appropriate sentences, for example 'I am a builder', 'I'd like to be a singer', or 'My mother/My father is . . .'

You might also do a lucky dip. Put all the items in a bag and have pupils pull one out and say what they would like to be according to what item they pull out of the bag, for example if they pull out the spanner, they would say 'I'd like to be a mechanic.' To give pupils more choice, they could be allowed to choose whether to use the positive or the negative, for example 'I would not like to be a mechanic.'

Many of the ideas of what to do with small items or flashcards can similarly be adapted.

Quizzes are a good way of motivating pupils to write down a large number of sentences as they will think of it as a game rather than just more writing. This activity may sound a bit chaotic but less able pupils in particular often get more written down than if they were just sitting in their places.

PREPARATION

Before pupils arrive, pin up around the room flashcards relevant to the topic(s) that you have been doing recently. Make sure you number them, either by writing on the card or by pinning a number to each card. Use about 20 cards to make the activity worthwhile and so as not to have too many pupils crowding around one card. I have often used 30 as this keeps pupils busy. If it is difficult to pin them up, then you can simply lay them out on tables.

ACTIVITY

Practise the appropriate language with pupils, making it clear what language you expect for each picture. Pictures of activities can require a separate sentence for each picture, for example 'I am swimming', 'I am playing tennis', whereas with nouns, you may wish pupils to use a particular phrase such as 'I would like an apple.' You may choose to use this activity to practise the past tense.

Then, if you have pinned up 20 cards, tell pupils to write down numbers 1–20 and explain exactly what sort of sentence you require for each picture. When you say 'Go', pupils get up from their seats and have to go around the room, writing down the 20 sentences. Reward the first pupil(s) to finish writing down all 20 sentences correctly and legibly.

Interview-style questions can be used in the teaching of any topic, from personal information or hobbies to availability and suitability for a summer holiday job.

PREPARATION

Make pairs of cards. On one card of each pair, you need a pen portrait of the person you are looking for and the questions the pupil will require to find this person. It is best for elementary learners for all the question cards to have the same questions so that you can drill them thoroughly in advance. More advanced learners can have different questions. On the second card of each pair write the answers, either as a cue in note form or in sentences for young learners. All answer cards should be different.

Elementary Card 1a

Details of the person you are looking for:

12 years old
birthday 22nd April
2 brothers
3 dogs
likes tennis

Questions to use:
How old are you?
When is your birthday?
Have you any brothers and sisters?
Have you any pets?
What sports do you like?

Elementary Card 1b

Here are the details that you must mention about yourself when you are interviewed:

I am 12
My birthday is 22nd April
I have two brothers
I have three dogs
I like tennis

Advanced Card 1a

You are looking for a student to work in your

1) hotel for
2) July/August
3) must speak English and French
4) must be 18
5) must have previous experience

Advanced Card 1b

You are an 18 year old student looking for hotel work for the summer. You are available for July, August and September. You speak English, French and Spanish and you worked in a hotel last year.

Ask various students the relevant questions until you find someone who can fulfil all five conditions above.

ACTIVITY

Give out one card to each pupil. Pupils then have to circulate, with the question-card pupils asking questions, until they find the pupil who has the correct pair card. You may find it best to give out question cards to all pupils on one side of the classroom and answer cards to those on the other side and explain to pupils that this is what you are doing.

WEATHER ACTIVITIES

WEATHER AND AN ACTIVITY

Use a weather flashcard and an activity flashcard to practise sentences such as 'When it's fine, I play tennis.' Pupils can come out to the front and pick one card from the weather pile and one from the activities and then make a sentence. A similar activity can be done with sets of small picture cards. Pupils can lay out sensible pairs of weather and activity and then write up their sentences.

MAP AND WEATHER

Use a map of the country and put various weather symbols in the different regions for the practising of sentences such as 'In the North it is cloudy.' This works particularly well with an OHT map and little bits of OHT acetate (mini acetates) with the various weather symbols, which can then be moved around the map, so as to encourage the use of different sentences. Weather can be practised in the past (what the weather was like yesterday or has been like today), present (habitual – what the climate is usually like) and future forecasts. Don't forget that some languages are spoken in more than one country and this is a good opportunity to use maps of a range of countries, particularly if they have very different climates.

You could also show a nightmare global-warming scenario saying what the weather will be like in 2100.

ANIMALS AND THE WEATHER

You can use animals to practise work on types of climate or simply to say who likes what sort of weather, for example frog – rain, polar bear – snow, lizard – sun, monkey – hot.

Practising language structures

Pretend that you have just emptied out your own or someone else's pockets/bag after a shopping trip, a day's excursion or a holiday, and lay out all the receipts and used tickets. To add to your own collection, ask around the staffroom for other people's rubbish! You can enlarge these on a photocopier to make individual flashcards of each receipt, you can arrange them in a specific order on a worksheet, or you can scan them into a computer and use the projected images. You can add a bit of interest to this activity by saying that they came out of your teenage son's pocket, your elderly mother's bag or that they were dropped by a celebrity. Alternatively you can ask the class to guess who might be the owner.

The aim of the activity is to say what the owner of the pocket/bag has been doing. You can link this activity to specific topics, such as:

o shopping (for food, clothes, leisure items)
o places in your local town (car park, post office)
o leisure activities (leisure centre, football match ticket, concert ticket)
o travel (bus, train, plane)
o famous city in the country of the target language (famous sights, cafes, etc.)
o eating and drinking (café and restaurant receipts for several occasions)

Use the stimulus material to practise sentences, such as:

o He/she/you went to town by bus . . .
o He/she/you went to the supermarket and you bought . . .
o He/she/you went to Fred's restaurant and you ate . . .

VARIATIONS
Some receipts have the time on them. You can add a time to the others. Then you can practise including a time in each sentence. If you put all the receipts onto a worksheet, you can ask pupils to put the activities into the correct order and write out the story from beginning to end.

FOLLOW-UP WRITTEN WORK

Pupils can write out an account of what they did on their last visit to town, or they can write about what a celebrity did on their shopping trip or holiday.

Pupils imagine that they are hosting a visitor from the target-language country. Show them a programme of activities for the week and tell them that they must make sure that their guest brings the right equipment with them each day.

Pupils are giving commands/reminders to each other about what to bring/take with them each day of the week.

- Monday – swimming
- Tuesday – walk in the country
- Wednesday – town
- Thursday – shopping
- Friday – sightseeing, then party
- Saturday – depart

For a very simple version, pupils make sentences by taking one phrase from each of columns 1, 2 and 3 below. A more challenging version would just have a list of items in column 2 and activities in column 3 with pupils having to supply the rest of the phrase themselves. The examples here are in the correct order, but you would provide the pupils with the items in a jumbled order so that they have to select the appropriate items.

1	2	3
On Monday	bring your swimming things	because you are going swimming
On Tuesday	bring your trainers	because you are going for a walk
On Wednesday	bring your town plan	because you will have free time in town
On Thursday	bring your money	because you are going shopping
On Friday	bring your smart clothes	because you are going straight to a party
On Saturday	bring all your luggage	because you are going home

This activity provides an opportunity to use language justifying decisions and explaining preferences. The traditional scenario for this game is that of a ship about to sink. Pupils imagine that they are getting into lifeboats and that they can only take with them ten items out of a longer list. They have to justify what they are taking with them, thinking about how they might survive in a lifeboat or what might be useful if they managed to find any land. A list of items to choose from could look something like this:

Torch, string, penknife, mobile phone, matches, warm clothes, a blanket, first aid kit, tins of food, water, tent, candles, flares, guitar, saucepan, the dog, a cup, a fishing rod

Pupils must make sentences such as 'We must/we ought to take a fishing rod to catch fish.'

Pupils can begin by each writing their own list of ten sentences, and then they could compare with other people in their group/class.

The same game can be played in a more realistic setting, such as:

1 deciding what to put in a suitcase to go on holiday
2 deciding what to put in a rucksack to go round the world.

You can provide pupils with lists of suggested items to choose from, or you can leave the task more open-ended with pupils trying to think of as complete a list as possible. Likewise you can set a maximum number of items such as 25 or leave it open-ended.

The holiday list to choose from could include a whole range of clothes and items such as sun-tan lotion, sunglasses, washing things, mobile phone and/or camera, passport, tickets, money.

The backpacking list could include the above plus camping equipment, water sterilization tablets, etc.

As an added complication, you could remind them that they need to keep the weight down.

BIRTHDAY BURGLARY!

This is a more exciting variation on the well-known game, Kim's game.

KIM'S GAME

Place a number of objects on a tray and practise saying what they are with the pupils. Then cover the tray with a cloth and remove one or more items. Then show pupils the tray again and ask them to say which items are missing. Repeat removing different items each time.

KIM'S GAME ON THE OVERHEAD PROJECTOR

Rather than using objects on a tray, it may be easier for pupils to see if you use separate little pictures in acetate on the OHP (see Idea 15, item 2). It is relatively easy to cover the OHP with a piece of paper or to switch off the OHP while you remove some pictures and move others around before you uncover the pictures again.

BIRTHDAY BURGLARY

You can do this on a worksheet, using two pictures of the same room in a house. Label the pictures 'Before the burglary' and 'After the burglary'. In the picture 'Before the burglary' include items such as TV, radio, etc. and omit them from the 'After the burglary' picture. Pupils then have to study the two pictures and say what is missing from the 'After the burglary' scene. Teach them the appropriate phrase that you want them to use, for example, 'The burglars have taken . . .'

On the OHP, you can have two separate pictures of before and after the burglary, and ask the pupils to say what is missing. Alternatively, you can use the greater versatility of the OHP to build up the story:

To do this, put a picture of the bare room on the OHP. Then use mini-acetates of the consumer goods (computer, mobile phone, clothes, etc.) and place these on the picture of the room, one by one, practising the vocabulary with the pupils. You can make up a story about someone receiving all these items for his/her birthday. Pupils can practise 'He/she received . . .'

Then sweep all the mini-acetates off the overhead projector, telling pupils that there has been a burglary and they then have to say what the burglars have taken, for example, 'The burglars have taken . . .'

For fun, you could include one ghastly present that not even the burglars have taken, such as an uncool item of clothing!

TIDY THAT ROOM!

Set the scene of Jason/Louise, the untidy teenager who leaves everything all over the bedroom.

Start with an overhead transparency of a teenage bedroom complete with teenager. Onto it place (one by one) mini-acetates of items of clothing, school things, plates, mugs, magazines, etc. (See Idea 15 for making mini-acetates.) As you place each item on the OHP, make pupils practise phrases such as: 'He/she has left the mug on the floor', 'He/she has left the T-shirt on the bed', etc.

Drill this language, by asking pupils 'Where has he/she left his/her . . . ?'

When you have covered the bedroom with mini-acetates, act the angry parent and say 'Tidy that room'.

Sweep all the mini-acetates off the OHP, and ask pupils 'What has Jason/Louise put away?' Pupils have to say 'He/she has put away . . .'

Alternatively sweep all the mini-acetates into a pile under the bed and pupils can practise: 'He/she has put . . . under the bed!'

See how many items pupils can remember.

The aim of this game is for pupils to work out what items they could afford and then to justify their choice. It also offers the opportunity to practise numbers and to become familiar with the currency of the country of the target language.

You will need a worksheet or overhead transparency with pictures of sports equipment with price tags on each one. If you do not have suitable pictures, you can use a written list of items. Make sure that the total of all the prices adds up to more than the prize money so that pupils cannot simply buy everything.

YOU HAVE WON £500 TO SPEND ON SPORTS EQUIPMENT

Set the scene by telling pupils that they have won some money to spend on sports equipment, but do not tell them how much just yet.

Start by showing them the pictures of the equipment in the sports shop and drilling the vocabulary for the items on display. Then practise together saying why they would like each item, for example, 'I would like . . . because . . .' Next practise saying the prices.

Then tell pupils that they have each won £500 to spend on the sports equipment. Show them the pictures or list of items that they can choose from. Ask pupils to write down the items they would choose and to write a sentence justifying their choice. Give them an example, such as: 'I would choose the football boots because I love football.'

Tell them they must keep within the budget you have set and give them a limited amount of time (e.g. 10 minutes) to write down their list and a sentence for each item. When the time is up, ask pupils to read out one of their sentences, saying what they would choose and why.

SPOILT FOR CHOICE – SPENDING PRIZE MONEY

LIVING ON A BUDGET

Pupils are told that they have a certain amount of money to spend on a particular project. This could be food for a party, furniture for a teenage bedroom or furnishings for a student bedsit.

Show the pupils visuals of the items on a worksheet or overhead transparency and drill the necessary vocabulary. Make sure each item also has a price tag. Give pupils the opportunity to ask the price and give the answer. Alternatively, you could do this by NOT putting the prices on the overhead transparency to begin with, but by laying on a blank overlay and writing the prices on as pupils ask you and you answer. Another way would be to use the blank overlay over the transparency of the items and then ask pupils to suggest to you how much each item would cost, e.g. 'A bottle of lemonade would be £1', 'A bedside lamp would be £10'.

When everything has a price, tell pupils how much the maximum they can spend is and ask them to write down what they would choose for their project and why. For example, I would get three bottles of lemonade because everyone likes lemonade. They could then work in pairs or groups and compare lists and come up with an agreed list between them.

Alternatively, pupils could be choosing items for a third party, for example a couple who are getting married, or a new baby in the family.

VERSION 1: 'WOULD YOU LIKE TO COME TO THE CINEMA WITH ME ON MONDAY EVENING?'

Practise the above sentence with pupils and revise the days of the week. Then practise ways of declining the offer and giving excuses. For example:

○ No, I'm sorry, I'm doing something else.
○ No, I'm sorry, I'm playing in a football match.
○ No, I'm sorry, I have to do my homework.

Get pupils to suggest as many different excuses as possible, revising leisure time vocabulary or vocabulary such as household tasks. Then ask the question and have the pupils decline.

You can work through the days of the week and ask a different pupil for each day. You can be more demanding by asking each pupil to give a different excuse from those already given. When pupils are thoroughly familiar with the language, then they can work in pairs with pupil A asking pupil B out each day of the week and pupil B declining each time with a different excuse.

VERSION 2: 'WHY DON'T WE . . .'

In this version, you vary the suggestions about what to do together. For example, 'Why don't we go shopping?', 'go to the match?', 'play tennis?', 'watch TV?'

Pupils' excuses can vary to express opinions: 'I don't want to do X because it's boring/tiring'. Again, after thorough class practice, pupils can make up dialogues in pairs.

VERSION 3: HOW SUBTLE IS THAT!

To add variety, pupils can suggest and practise different types of excuses, ranging from the polite excuse which would not hurt anyone's feelings to a very blunt answer such as 'No, I'm sorry, I'm going to the film with someone else'. Pupils can then make up dialogues in pairs, perhaps starting with subtle excuses and finishing with something more blunt.

WHAT COULD HAVE HAPPENED?

The aim of this activity is to practise saying what you think might have happened.

Scenario 1: Your friend (or a celebrity) is late for an appointment. Suggest why.

For less advanced pupils, reasons could be expressed as simple past tense statements such as 'The bus was late/He got up late', etc. More advanced pupils could use structures such as 'He may have had an accident'. Possible explanations can vary from the mundane to the more far-fetched, from 'He may have thought we said 3pm not 2pm' to 'He may have been kidnapped'.

Scenario 2: You are evacuated from a shop in an emergency. You and your friends are wondering what might have happened.

o 'There may have been a bomb scare'
o 'There may have been a gunman threatening a cashier'
o 'Someone may have set off a fire alarm'

Suggestions might include power failure, flood, fire, terrorist threat, staff shortage, staff walk out, gas escape, someone taken ill, dangerous animal on the rampage, people fighting over bargains in a sale.

Practise the language needed to

○ describe a person
○ describe what a place looks like
○ say what happened

Show pupils one picture or a sequence of several pictures showing the scene of a crime, e.g.:

○ picture 1: a window display in a jewellers
○ picture 2: a couple of suspicious-looking characters
○ picture 3: the aftermath of a crime (window empty, broken glass)

As you show each picture, drill the appropriate vocabulary (e.g. jewellery, language for describing people).

Then remove the picture(s) from sight and ask the pupils to write down an eye-witness account describing the suspects and the crime scene.

You can repeat the activity in another lesson, using slightly different pictures (different shop and suspects). For variation, you could have a dog in a butcher's.

WITNESS AT A CRIME SCENE

The aim of this activity is to practise saying what is missing from the picture, using phrases such as 'He/she has lost his/her . . .' or 'His/her leg is missing'.

BROKEN STATUES

Make a worksheet, overhead transparency or flashcards out of pictures of broken statues (or find pictures of complete statues and erase limbs off them). Pupils say sentences such as 'He/she has lost her head' or 'His/her head is missing'.

ACTIVITY PICTURES

Use familiar visuals, showing people doing tasks, that you have used to teach activities such as hobbies or household chores. From each picture, erase the equipment that they are using (e.g. tennis racquet/violin/ vacuum cleaner). Revise the activities and make sure that everyone is clear about what each person is doing. Then practise saying what item is missing from each picture.

Find two pictures showing the same room or rooms in a house. One picture should be of the present day and the other of sometime in the past (e.g. 1940s, 1800 or medieval times). History colleagues may be able to help you find suitable pictures. The kitchen or the living room will probably provide you with the most vocabulary to practise.

Contrast the two pictures, using sentences such as

In 1940 there was no . . .   *Now there is . . .*
In 1940 they did not have . . .   *Now we have . . .*

Depending on what date your historical picture is, items you might contrast could include electricity, kitchen appliances, radio, TV, telephone, music equipment. If you wish you could have pictures representing several different eras.

FOLLOW-UP WRITTEN WORK
Pupils could then write a description of the room in the present and the one in the past

ROOM OF THE FUTURE
As an extension activity, or on another occasion when you are dealing with the future tense, pupils could design a room or a house for the future and write a description of it using the future tense.

Bring in a collection of items that have been found in someone's bag/pockets. Begin by making sure the class all know what the items are and what they are called in the target language. Then use the items to ask the class what we know about the person from the contents of their bag/pockets, for example:

o Cigarettes – he smokes
o Chocolate wrapper – he likes chocolate
o Car keys – he drives a car
o Receipt – he buys . . .
o Concert ticket – he goes to listen to . . .
o Dog's lead – he has a dog

With more advanced learners, you can use this activity to practise degrees of uncertainty with structures such as: 'He probably smokes', 'he may have eaten some chocolate . . .'

FOUND ON A CORPSE
If you want to be a bit more macabre, you can imagine that the items were found on a murder victim. This gives you the opportunity to practise using the past tense to say what he/she did. Again, more advanced learners can hypothesize about what he/she might have done and what might have happened. They can even differentiate what they think the victim definitely did and what they think he/she might have done.

Great games

Use this to teach geographical vocabulary: hill, beach, forest, port, lake, river, etc.; directions: right/left; or position words: in front of, next to, near . . . and/or compass points.

Preparation: make three OHTs, the first, OHT1, being a map of a treasure island complete with geographical features (mountain, forest, etc.); the second, OHT2, being an overlay which is made by laying a blank OHT over the treasure island OHT1 and writing in the new vocabulary (mountain, etc.) in the correct place; the third, OHT3, just has the outline of the island and a cross (or treasure chest if you can draw) to show where the treasure is. Hide this OHT3 in an envelope. You may also need a blank OHT4 to write pupils' initials on (see 3 and 5).

1 Put OHT1 on the OHP and put OHT2 on top of it. Practise the geographical features vocabulary first with the overlay OHT2 in place and then without it.
2 Practise whatever directions/position words you intend to exploit.
3 Start the game by getting pupils to put their hands up and tell you where they think the treasure is (left/west of the river, next to the lake). Mark the spot with the pupil's initials. You can do this on OHT4.
4 When finished build up a bit of suspense and excitement as you get OHT3 out of its envelope and place it on the OHP over the OHT1 (and over OHT4 if you are using it), taking care to match up the coastline of OHT1 and OHT3 so everyone can see where the treasure is and which pupil has got the nearest. It is important that the pupils can see that the treasure OHT3 was prepared before and comes out of an envelope so it does not look as if you have just decided where the treasure is and risk accusations of fix or favouritism.
5 Be ready for pupils to demand a second game – often better to save this for next lesson as variety is also important. The winner can be allowed to draw the treasure on for next time.

Find the treasure in an abandoned city, or find a cat or
baby after an earthquake.

You can use this activity to teach buildings around
town – town hall, station, church, school, various shops,
supermarket, etc. – and directions, including first, second
on the left/right, and location words such as opposite.

This activity uses the same idea as the treasure island
activity described on the previous page but the scenario
is either an abandoned city (for example Pompeii or an
Inca settlement), which can include some rather
anachronistic buildings(!), with the task being to find the
treasure or, if you prefer to avoid the anachronistic, then
we might imagine our cat went off wandering around our
modern town just before an earthquake and now we're
trying to find it.

Make up the OHTs as for treasure island, but this
time OHT1 is a town plan with streets and buildings
(tourist brochure or internet sites could provide you
with a map), OHT2 has the names of buildings, and
OHT3 has the treasure/cat.

Use this activity to teach the verbs 'to live' or 'to be', and the floors of a block of flats. This can then be adapted to teach words such as door, window, balcony or rooms in the house.

PREPARATION

1   Find a large cardboard box such as a banana box, which is about one metre long and about 70 cm wide. The depth is unimportant.

2   Stand the box on its end so that the bottom of the box is now the front of your block of flats. Draw on floors (e.g., basement, ground floor, 1st floor, etc.) complete with balcony, windows (and shutters if appropriate for the country whose language you are teaching).

3   Make the windows (or shutters) so that they open and close.

4   Decide what you are going to use as inhabitants – glove puppets, soft toys, pictures of celebrities (you can stick pictures of the heads of celebrities on cardboard and put these on sticks or straws).

LANGUAGE PRACTICE

1   Place the box somewhere so that it is clearly visible to the class (e.g., on top of a filing cabinet).

2   Introduce the vocabulary – basement, ground floor, etc. – using the box.

3   Poke a glove puppet through a window to say, for example, 'The cat lives on the second floor' or 'Homer Simpson lives . . .' Repeat with other characters on other floors.

TOM AND JERRY VERSION

Just use two glove puppets who appear at different windows. Use the question 'Where is X?' or 'Is X on the 1st floor?' If you use a cat and a mouse glove puppet or stick puppet, with a bit of practice you can do a chase with the mouse appearing on one floor and then the cat.

HOUSE VERSION OR FLOORS/DEPARTMENTS IN
A BIG DEPARTMENT STORE

You can make another cardboard box into a house to teach
the floors and rooms but you should give some indication
of what the rooms are on the outside of the house (e.g., one
window which opens and another window through which
you can see a bit of the room). Likewise for teaching the
different departments in a department store.

IDEA
57

CLUEDO

This is a whole-class version of the game Cluedo in which players have to solve a murder mystery, finding out where, by whom and with what the murder was committed.

PREPARATION

You need a plan of a house on OHT and 12 small rectangles about 4 cm × 3 cm of OHT acetate. Make six of these into the suspected persons. I keep the people as simply Mr/Mrs (and have used a top-hat symbol to show which are Mr) and use simple colours (red, blue, etc.) but pupils may ask you for the Cluedo names (Colonel Mustard, Miss Scarlet, etc.). On each of the other six rectangles of acetate draw a weapon (I usually try just to teach knife, rope and revolver but pupils who know the game invariably ask for candlestick, spanner and lead piping so have these ready, although these words are unlikely to be on the syllabus).

HOW TO PLAY

1   Give each pupil a blank slip of paper on which they must secretly write the name of: one room, one person and one weapon. Ask them to fold over their piece of paper and collect up the pieces of paper and put them in a box. Pull one out, look at it but don't say what's on it.

2   Pupils then put their hands up to guess which room it says. As pupils guess, you can cross off the rooms they mention and then tick the correct one. Reward the pupil who gets the correct answer with a point.

3   Pupils then have to guess the person (Mr Green, etc.). You can line up the six persons along the side of the OHP so they are visible and, as the pupils guess them, move the wrong guesses out of sight. When the correct guess is made, move that person into the correct room. Reward the correct guess.

4   Repeat (3) with the weapon.

5   Start again, having rubbed out any marks on the rooms. One of the winning pupils can pick out a piece of paper from the box and say yes or no to pupils' guesses.

Use this activity to teach phrases such as 'You are nice', and to practise numbers. You can also use it for fortune-telling language 'You are going to travel . . .'

Although easy to make this is quite difficult to explain. There are many websites which lay out instructions as to how to make the fortune teller, one of the best is – http://www.enchantedlearning.com/crafts/origami/fortuneteller

HOW TO MAKE A FORTUNE TELLER

1 Give each pupil a square piece of paper, or an A4 sheet and show them how to make a square by folding down one corner and tearing off the end strip.
2 Fold the four corners of the square to the middle to make a new square.
3 Turn the paper over and again fold the four new corners to the middle.
4 Fold this square in half to make a rectangle, unfold and fold in half the other way.
5 Now insert your thumbs and forefingers into the flaps created and bring them together towards the middle. You should now have created the mechanisms of the fortune teller.
6 On the outside of the fortune teller write the numbers one to eight in the target language
7 On the inside, on each separate triangle, write a colour.
8 Under each triangle the student should write a phrase such as 'you are' + adjective or 'you are going to' + activity.

PLAYING FORTUNE TELLERS

Once pupils have written their sentences into the fortune teller, they can circulate, working in pairs to tell each other's fortunes.

Pupil A: 'Pick a number.' (Pupil B has to pick from those on the outside of the fortune teller.)

Pupil B: 'Five.'

Pupil A then opens and shuts the fortune teller five times and shows the inside to Pupil B who then chooses one of the four colours showing.

Pupil A then opens the flap and reads out the fortune under the colour chosen.

Ideal for teaching the narration of past events.

GROUPING PUPILS

Pupils need to be in groups of 4–6. A quick way to put pupils into fours is to ask two pupils to turn round to work with the two pupils behind them.

Each pupil needs a sheet of A4 paper and they must conceal whatever they write on the paper from the other pupils.

It can be useful to use a writing frame on the board or OHT to help pupils. The sections in brackets are the pupils' free choice, although you may wish to guide them with ideas.

1 (boy's name) met
2 (girl's name)
3 at/in (name of place)
4 on (date or day of the week)
5 He said (. . .)
6 She said (. . .)
7 They (action they did)
8 The consequence was . . .

THE GAME

Ask the pupils to write a boy's name on the paper and then turn down the top of the paper to conceal what they have written.

Then they should pass their piece of paper to the person on their left in their group. The recipient of the paper must not unfold it but must write down a girl's name on the paper. They must not write on the flap but on the sheet of paper itself so that all the writing ends up on the same side of the paper. They then fold the paper over again and pass it to their left. The process is repeated for all eight items. Then, at the end, unfold the paper and read them out to the class. The teacher can read the first few to make sure the pupils know what language to use and then pupils can volunteer to read theirs out.

CONSEQUENCES

The game assassin encourages speaking and writing in the past tense. Although it seems a bit complicated to set up, writing the cards will not take you long as you can copy and edit so much of them. While the speaking activity described on this page is an excellent activity on its own, you may also like to follow it up with the pupils writing their own version. You will find instructions for this on the next page.

PREPARATION

Pupils work in groups of four, one detective and three suspects, so you need as many sets of four cards as you have groups of four pupils, i.e. seven sets for a class of 28. As you go around to each group and give out the cards, ask each group to choose an intelligent person to be the detective. To the detective, you give card one which has details of the crime and cues for the questions to ask the suspects. It is important that the detective does not show this card to other members of the group. The three suspects each have a card with cues to say how they spent the evening, one of which has information which betrays him/her to the detective (for example the perfume/after-shave they were wearing, what they drank).

HOW TO PLAY

The detective asks the suspects the questions in order to work out which suspect carried out the murder. The best group involvement is achieved if the detective asks each suspect question one and then each suspect question two and so on until, on asking the last few questions, they discover who the murderer is.

I have found that with school-aged pupils you get better practise of the whole sentence said correctly in the past tense by giving them the whole sentence to say. This also then acts as a model for the second part of the activity when the pupils write their own version.

Card 1 ○ The Detective

You are the detective. Here are the murder details. Ask all the suspects the questions below to find the murderer.

Last night there was a murder committed at about 11.30pm in a café in the Boulevard St Michel in Paris. Near the corpse they found an ace of hearts (playing card), black dog hairs and red wine stains.

1. What time did you leave the house last night?
2. Where did you go last night.
3. How did you get to the Café Rouge?
4. What did you eat?
5. What did you drink?
6. What did you do in the café?
7. What time did you leave the café?
8. Did you go straight home?
9. Did you go to the café alone? Or with whom?

Card 2 ○ A suspect

When the detective asks you questions, these are your replies.

1. I left the house at 9pm
2. I went to the Café Rouge in the Boulevard St Michel.
3. I went to the café by motorbike.
4. I ate a hotdog.
5. I drank red wine.
6. I played table football.
7. I left the café at midnight.
8. No, I went to a club.
9. I went to the café and the club with three friends

Card 3 ○ A suspect

When the detective asks you questions, these are your replies.

1. I left the house at nine thirty.
2. I went to the Café Rouge in the Boulevard St Michel.
3. I went on foot.
4. I ate a hamburger and chips.
5. I drank red wine.
6. I played cards and I watched TV.
7. I left the café at 11.45pm.
8. I went straight home.
9. I went to the café with my black dog.

Card 4 ○ A suspect

When the detective asks you questions, these are your replies.

1. I left the house at 10pm.
2. I went to the Café Rouge in the Boulevard St Michel.
3. I went to the café by bike.
4. I ate a cheese sandwich.
5. I drank a beer.
6. I watched TV and I played cards.
7. I left the café at 1am.
8. No, I went to a club.
9. I went to the café and the club with two friends.

Figure 1: A set of sample cards for the assassin game

This is a follow-on activity for pupils to do when they have played the assassin game described on the last page.

I have found this to be one of the best ways to get pupils to say and write simple sentences in the past tense, particularly as they really like writing versions for each other and playing each other's versions.

When pupils have played the assassin game, make sure they realize how the activity works (i.e. that most of what the suspects do should be the same with the telling differences kept for the last couple of questions). They can then write their own version, either in groups or alone, with a view to giving it to another group to do. Suggest they think of what the giveaway factor is going to be before they start writing. Remind them to keep their voices down as they will be passing their finished version on to another group to solve afterwards and so they should be wary of giving the game away. To produce accurate language, they would be well-advised to stick closely to your model to start with. You can organize it so that they give in their versions to you and you correct them before they are used in the next lesson by another group. I have also made them write their original version on rough, lined paper, taken them in and corrected them and then made the pupils write out a neat correct version on smart-looking card. We have then played the game again in our class using their versions and we have also 'sent' our cards to be used by another parallel class and received their versions back in return. This way pupils have repeated time after time those basic past tense sentences such as I went, I ate, I drank, etc.

During this activity pupils can practise descriptions, lost-property language, personal details, hobbies and professions.

SCENARIO

A bag has been found with certain items in it, but several people claim it is theirs. To start with you can be the lost property officer and the class those looking for their bag. Ask a number of pupils their name, address and date of birth and then show the class an item from the bag such as a library card with those details on which shows that the bag must belong to that person.

IN GROUPS

If groups of four there should be one lost-property officer and three people who claim the bag is theirs. The lost property officer can be given a bag with the items in it and a card with questions. The questions can simply use descriptive language about the items in the bag such as 'What colour is your mobile phone?' or personal information language such as 'What's your address?' Alternatively they can be much more devious, using information on things like train tickets, 'Where did you go by train?', depending on what sort of language you want to teach. The other three members of the group who claim that the bag is theirs have their answer cards which either have sentence cues, one-word cues or picture cues that they use to answer the lost property officer.

PRACTICE IN MAKING UP QUESTIONS

Most learners find it much more difficult to make up questions than to answer the questions that their teacher asks them. Another use of this activity can simply be to display the items found in the bag at the front of the classroom and ask pupils to write down questions which could be used to check if the person claiming the bag was likely to be the real owner. This activity could focus very narrowly on one structure, e.g. using a range of sports equipment such as a tennis ball, a golf ball, a squash racket, a football and a table tennis bat to encourage pupils to write down five questions such as 'Do you play tennis?', etc., or it can be more open-ended, encouraging pupils to form a range of questions.

WHOSE BAG IS IT?

Each group/pair has an envelope in which there are
pictures and a number of cards with sentences on them.

1 The pupils must lay the cards out on the table in
front of them and match the pictures to the
sentences. You can put in more sentences than there
are pictures, for example a picture of a boat, one card
which says 'we went by boat' and one which says 'we
went by plane'. If you do this, then tell the pupils to
put the 'wrong' cards out of the way in the envelope.
2 They should put the cards into a logical order.
3 They copy out the sentences to form a narrative
including all the pictures (e.g., plane, hotel, beach,
souvenirs, café). This activity can be as easy or
difficult as you make the pictures.

Here are some suggestions:

PICTURES	SENTENCES
A calendar with a ring around 5–12th August	We left on 5 August
An aeroplane/airport	We went by plane
A hotel	We stayed in a hotel
Beach	We went to the beach
Café	We ate an ice-cream in a café
Souvenirs with price labels	We bought souvenirs

This activity is similar to the preceding Idea. However, instead of having words and sentences in an envelope, pupils only have pictures in the envelope. They then have to find the appropriate language from their previous work. They can be instructed to write at least one or two sentences per picture.

SAME OR DIFFERENT ENVELOPE CONTENTS FOR EACH PAIR
Envelopes with the same contents are the easiest to prepare for a whole class. However, producing several different versions (e.g., skiing holiday, beach holiday, city holiday) means that as soon as pupils have finished off one story, they can have another envelope to write another story. If you plan to do this, always have more envelopes than pairs as otherwise you will find that there is a traffic jam with no new envelope available for those who are the quickest to finish. You can of course make envelopes of varying difficulty to use in mixed-ability classes.

HOLIDAY SNAPS: DIFFICULT VERSION

Active listening

IDEA

65

MONSTERS

You can use this as a listening activity to practise parts of the body and numbers. You can also use adjectives such as long, thin, short, fat, hairy.

PREPARATION

Give a small blank rectangle of paper to each pupil (e.g., a piece of A4 cut into four, or use little squares from a message pad).

ACTIVITY

You make statements about a monster, for example 'It has two heads' and, in response to each statement you make, pupils have to draw a monster according to your description (two heads, one eye, three legs, etc.). At the end, they put their names on the back. Collect up and eliminate any which show miscomprehension, such as the wrong number of limbs. Then give the remainder to a colleague to judge and award a prize for best monster. It is much better to use a monster rather than a person as you do not have to be good at drawing to draw a monster whereas many pupils would be put off, thinking that they are no good at drawing people. Telling pupils in advance that their monsters will be judged encourages them to make an effort and they find this activity much more interesting than an ordinary listening exercise.

This activity can be used for topics such as a plan of a house, flat, school, shopping street, town or campsite. As well as the topic-specific vocabulary, such as the names of the shops, it can use left/right or position words such as opposite, next to, in between.

PREPARATION

Give pupils either simply a blank sheet or a quick outline they can copy from the board. This might be a shopping street with five shops on each side and one shop already named. Easy outlines can be done for a flat, a house, a part of a school or a department store. If you prefer, you can obviously duplicate much more elaborate outlines such as town plans based on real towns in tourist brochures with the key buildings blanked out and replaced with numbers.

ACTIVITY 1 – ONE INSTRUCTION AT A TIME

Give one instruction at a time and pupils have to write in the word in the correct place. So, for example, you may have a street with a baker's shop in it and you say 'The greengrocer's shop is on the left of the baker's.'

ACTIVITY 2 – FOR BUDDING ARCHITECTS OR TOWN PLANNERS

Give a series of instructions such as 'In this campsite, the shop must be near the entrance', 'The showers must be next to the toilets'. Pupils have to note down these instructions and then they have to draw an appropriate plan and label it. Pupils can do this individually or in pairs or groups.

DRAWING A HOUSE

IDEA

67

WHO IN THE CLASS HAS . . . ?

A useful listening exercise for practising descriptions and for teaching the words girl/boy or getting pupils to hear the difference between he and she, as so often classroom dialogue tends to focus on I/you.

PREPARATION
Pupils need paper or exercise books to jot down the answers.

ACTIVITY
Ask the pupils to write 1–5 (or however many you are going to do) in the margin and then begin with your first statement such as 'Name a boy who has short, blond hair', 'Name a girl who wears glasses' and have pupils write down the name of a fellow pupil. There will often be more than one correct answer. Alternatively you can say 'he has . . .' or 'she has . . .' and pupils need to listen out for he/she as well as the description. Some more adventurous pupils might like to be the 'teacher' and say the next sentence and so they say the cue sentence and pupils all write down an answer. When checking through the answers, you can ask pupils to make a whole sentence so that instead of just saying Jane, they have to say 'Jane has short, brown hair.' Likewise you can do follow-up written work in which pupils have to write out a sentence for each of the names they have jotted down. Make sure that they have the appropriate model sentences 'He has . . .' and 'She has . . .' and the appropriate vocabulary to complete this part of the activity.

In language learning we often forget how important it is for pupils to hear new words a number of times before we ask them to say the words. We can find ourselves rushing on to make pupils say new words before they have had time to absorb the sounds and meanings of these words.

In these activities pupils concentrate on listening and they show their comprehension through actions. The reasoning behind these activities is that even well-behaved children will daydream, and it is much better if they actually have to do something that the teacher can see them doing in order to show they are following the lesson.

In the following games pupils all stand up and when they are eliminated (i.e. 'out') they sit down. Pupils can be eliminated for the wrong action or being the last one to get to the correct action. To maximize practice for as many pupils as possible, try to get very few pupils out near the beginning and then, perhaps by making the activity more difficult or by speeding up, get a lot more out just before the end. I have found one way of avoiding just having a few pupils in for a long time at the end with other pupils getting bored is to say that you will time the whole game for two minutes and all pupils who are still in at the end automatically get a point. This means that everyone has a chance of winning a point.

TRUE/FALSE STATEMENTS

Pupils must put their thumbs up to signify true and turn their thumbs down to signify false. This activity can be used with any topic. It can be used with flashcards so that you hold up, for example, a picture of a fish but say 'It's a horse'.

SIMON SAYS . . .

FINGER NUMBERS

When you say a number, pupils have to put up that number of fingers. Can be used for numbers 1–10 or can be adapted for 10, 20, 30.

TURN LEFT/TURN RIGHT/GO STRAIGHT ON

Pupils have to put their arms out to the left, the right or straight on in response to your commands. This can be made more complicated by having to use fingers of the correct hand to show 1st, 2nd, 3rd. Thus if you say 3rd on the right, pupils have to hold out their right arm and hold up three fingers of their right hand.

TOUCH YOUR . . . PARTS OF THE BODY, OR CLOTHES

You say 'touch your head' or 'touch your shoes' and pupils have to touch the relevant item.

SIMON SAYS

A well-known variation on the above in which pupils must only carry out the action if you say 'Simon says' at the beginning. So if you say 'Simon says touch your nose' then pupils must do so but if you omit the 'Simon says' then pupils must not do the action. Find out what the target language version of this activity is.

POINT TO THE PICTURE IN THE BOOK

Pupils all have a textbook open at the correct page and must point to the correct picture in the book when the teacher says a word or sentence which is relevant to that picture. This may be better done simply as an activity rather than a game as it is not very practical to eliminate pupils while doing this activity unless it is a very small class or you ask pupils to watch each other and point out who is out (though this can lead to arguments). One way to add a bit of competitive edge to this activity is for each pair of pupils to share a textbook and to compete with each other to be the first to touch the correct picture. Even without any scoring system, pupils seem to enjoy trying to be the first to touch the picture.

STAND UP IF . . .

If you play this as a game in which pupils are already standing up then you can say 'Put your hand up if . . . ' You can make up sentences about physical appearance such as 'Stand up if you have blue eyes', or about other things such as brothers/sisters/hobbies/when their birthday is, for example 'Stand up if you play football for the school', 'Stand up if your birthday is in May', 'Stand up if you have three sisters'. It may be best done as a non-competitive game unless you can be sure of your facts.

POINT TO THE PICTURE

GET YOUR FACTS RIGHT

This can be used for topics such as personal information or members of the family.

You can often make topics more interesting and more relevant by using up-to-date factual information in your listening exercises. The fact that pupils may already know some of the answers in their own language often motivates them to listen keenly. Items which lend themselves to this type of activity include:

o football scores
o dates of birth of famous people
o relationships/relatives: 'x has three children'
o descriptions of famous people
o simple news headlines for more advanced students

This activity can be done as a simple exercise or as a quiz, with pupils working individually or in pairs.

You describe a person in the class and the pupils have to write down who it is. Once you have established what to do, you can ask pupils to volunteer to describe someone in the class. This is a good way of stretching some of the more able pupils while other pupils are simply doing a comprehension exercise.

You can also do this activity with other people who are known to the pupils, such as members of staff or famous people. This allows you to use more adult vocabulary such as bald, beard or moustache. You need to make sure that everyone knows these people. One way to make the activity more accessible is to put up a list of people from whom pupils choose. You do not need to give a whole description of one person at a time. Instead you can say one sentence for one question and then say another sentence about the same person later on as a different question.

If pupils do not guess who you are talking about straight away, encourage them to make notes so that they can return to the question later. Then give pupils a few minutes at the end to fill in or guess any answers they have not completed.

As a follow-up activity pupils could write a statement about each of the people mentioned or they could use the appropriate vocabulary to make up further questions which you could use in a similar exercise or quiz at a later date.

This listening exercise consists of the teacher giving pupils a list of categories in the target language and how many items of each category they must write down. When pupils have written down this list, they then have to write down the items required. This is a good end of unit or end of year activity.

Your list might look like this:

a   five colours
b   ten numbers
c   five animals
d   six nationalities
e   four members of the family
f   twelve months
g   seven days of the week
h   ten school subjects
i   three opinions
j   ten sports
k   six hobbies that are not sports
l   eight places to go around the town
m   four rooms in the house
n   six items of furniture

Creative writing

This activity can be used to practise some or all of the following:

1 the names of town-centre buildings, shops;
2 home and work places: block of flats, house, factory, office;
3 services: school, hospital, police station, fire station;
4 geographical features, such as near the sea, on a river, near the mountains;
5 location words: near to, far from;
6 transport facilities, such as motorway, airport, railway station, bus station, cycle tracks, car park;
7 leisure and entertainment facilities, such as park, sports' ground, leisure centre, youth club, cinema.

PREPARATION
A blank A3 sheet of paper for each pair/group. Little picture cards of places around the town or a list of facilities to be included/excluded. Vocabulary lists accessible for other words pupils might want.

DEMONSTRATION
Use the board/OHP to show pupils how they might draw on a coastline, river, motorway and then place on the buildings.

ACTIVITY
Pupils work in groups or pairs. Pupils have to draw features such as the sea, hills, roads, railways, etc., onto the A3 sheet and then lay out picture cards with shops, leisure centre, houses, etc., in a way that seems ideal to them. They label the features in the target language. Set a time limit by when they must have finished, or some pupils would take all day drawing and not get on to the writing. They can then write up an account of their ideal town. At the simplest level, this can include 'In my ideal town there are . . . (a list of nouns)'. At a more advanced stage, pupils could use phrases such as 'In my ideal town I would like . . ., there would be . . ., one could have. . .'

FOLLOW-UP WORK

You can do some oral work with questions such as 'In your town is there a . . .?' or 'Where is the . . .?' or you can allow pupils to walk around to see what the other groups have done.

Using the same idea as the ideal town, pupils can be given a blank piece of paper and some picture cards as starters to help them design their ideal school, house, bedroom or holiday. If some of these items are rather beyond the scope of your usual coursebook materials, then try using glossy magazines or the internet. For some items you may find it useful to write a phrase by the picture to make it clear what the picture is supposed to be or to give pupils the appropriate vocabulary, for example 'a computer with lots of games'.

Pictures could include:

IDEAL SCHOOL
Sports' centre, swimming pool, bar, cinema, theatre, recording studios.

IDEAL HOUSE
Expensive car for the garage, remote control for the gate/garage, games room, children's TV room, music recording studio, sports' facilities, for example tennis courts, swimming pool, jacuzzi, beauty salon, bar/restaurant, luxury bathroom, lift, automatic doors.

IDEAL BEDROOM
Computer with lots of games, wardrobe with lots of clothes or wardrobe for each colour, drum kit, robot to tidy up.

IDEAL HOLIDAY
Exotic location pictures, desert island, moon, Hollywood, etc., and

o pictures of the activities that your pupils might like to do on their ideal holiday where cost is no object: jet skiing, scuba diving, hang-gliding, bungee jumping;
o pictures of hotel facilities similar to those used for the ideal house or the ideal bedroom;
o pictures of luxury transport: helicopter, Porsche, rocket;
o pictures of celebrities they would like to meet.

VARIATIONS (WORK PARTICULARLY WELL FOR IDEAL HOLIDAYS)

Pictures are spread out on several large surfaces around the classroom and pupils (or one pupil from each group) have to collect eight (for example) pictures in a set time and then use those pictures on their plan of their ideal item. They then have to write out their description/account.

HOMEWORK

Pupils have to bring in their own pictures, for example ask them to bring seven pictures about an ideal holiday. These could be pictures that pupils find in newspapers, magazines or on the internet. Alternatively pupils could draw simple pictures.

COMPARING MONSTERS

This activity is useful for practising comparative structures and adjectives.

PREPARATION

Make your own version of two monsters on OHT which you can show pupils. Prepare vocabulary lists if needed – it is often handy for pupils to have a lot of different adjectives that they might use, and, if relevant to the language you are teaching, lists of irregular comparatives.

ACTIVITY

Tell pupils they have to draw two monsters, give each monster a name and then write ten sentences comparing them. Pupils can often make up more sentences by saying something the opposite way round, for example 'X is taller than Y' and 'Y is shorter than X'. You can limit the activity to one comparative structure such as 'X is more elegant than Y' or you can include 'X is less fierce than Y', 'X is as funny as Y', 'X is not as happy as Y'.

PORTRAIT OF A CELEBRITY

This can either be done at a form-filling level or as an exercise in writing a paragraph from a form.

FORM-FILLING – WRITING A FACTSHEET

Pupils use a magazine article as a reading comprehension exercise from which they extract the necessary details to fill in the factsheet. It is rare that you will find an article which is at exactly the correct linguistic level so it is often easier to write your own version from an article or a factsheet. The Internet can be a useful source of the necessary information. After all doing the same one as an example, you can have a choice of follow-up worksheets available, for example one sheet with several footballers, one sheet with several soap stars, one sheet with several members of a band.

Surname:	First name:
Date of birth:	Place of birth:
Eye colour:	Hair colour:
Brothers and sisters: (or family)	Successes: (roles played/ goals scored)
Hobbies:	Favourite colour:

PARAGRAPH WRITING

Pupils can use the information gathered in their factsheet and present in paragraph form, with sentences such as 'he has . . . eyes', 'he was born in . . . ', etc.

HOMEWORK

More highly motivated pupils can be encouraged to bring in their own information from magazines or the Internet to use in a future lesson to produce a similar factsheet or paragraph.

WALL-DISPLAY

Pupils like seeing pictures of their idols on the walls so this activity lends itself well to a wall-display with pupils either producing handwritten or computer-typed versions for the wall, together with pictures.

IDEA

78

HOROSCOPES

Before undertaking this activity in a school, check that there are not going to be any objections to you using horoscopes. In favour of this activity, you can say that by showing that anyone can write a horoscope, you actually demonstrate to pupils that there is no truth in them.

STIMULUS MATERIAL

1 Magazine page with horoscopes in the target language. These are often very difficult, covering a wide range of vocabulary but actually seeing horoscopes in the target language acts as an inspiration for pupils. At the very least, pupils can recognize the signs of the zodiac and then use the names and the dates for their own version. Underline the more accessible phrases for pupils and list these underneath as useful vocabulary.

2 Prepare lists of appropriate language structures and vocabulary that pupils are likely to want, as otherwise you will find yourself inundated with requests for how to say things. Decide what structures you want pupils to use, for example 'you are going to . . .' or 'you will . . .' and what sort of vocabulary would be useful.

Your list might include

You will meet	+ nouns, such as an interesting person,
You will receive	some money, bad news, good news
You will win	some money
You will go to	a location
You will have to	+ make a decision
You will be successful in	+ work, romance, school, money matters
You will have bad luck in	

ACTIVITY

You can introduce the activity by going through the magazine horoscope reading the underlined phrases with pupils. Pupils can then write their own. You can limit this to one sentence per sign or be more open-ended.

The environment is a topic which is now included in many an exam syllabus, but it often involves introducing rather a lot of specific vocabulary. As one way of introducing or reinforcing this vocabulary, you can use this comprehension exercise.

Provide each group/pair of pupils with an envelope containing pieces of card each with a sentence about the state of the environment in 50 years' time. Pupils then have to sort out the ideas into optimistic and pessimistic predictions, and copy them into their books. Your statements could include:

PESSIMISTIC PREDICTIONS

It will be hotter because of global warming.
There will be more hurricanes and floods.
There will be more deserts.
There will be more pollution.
There will be more traffic.
Many species of animal will disappear.
Many types of plant will disappear.
Many trees will die because of acid rain.

OPTIMISTIC PREDICTIONS

There will be more electricity generated from renewable
    sources.
There will be hydrogen cars which do not cause
    pollution.
Everyone will recycle more things.
Houses will have better insulation.

WHAT WILL THE PLANET EARTH
BE LIKE IN 50 YEARS' TIME?

CURRENT AFFAIRS

Developing on from the previous idea you could ask pupils to consider topics which cover a broader range of current affairs. Statements could include:

PESSIMISTIC PREDICTIONS
There will be more famine and disease.
There will be more terrorism.
There will be more wars.

OPTIMISTIC PREDICTIONS
Scientists will find a cure for AIDS.
Everyone will have enough to eat.
There will be less racism.
Poor countries will become richer.

To provide pupils with practice of the appropriate structures and vocabulary, you can start with a series of questions which pupils can answer by manipulating the question sentence. You can do these questions orally and then ask pupils to write down the answers, for example: In 10 years' time . . .

1   how old will you be?
2   will you be studying or working?
3   what will you be studying or what will you be doing as a job?
4   will you be living with your parents or independently?
5   will you be living in this country or abroad?
6   will you have children?
7   what will you be doing in your free time?
8   where will you be going on holiday?
9   will you stay in touch with your current friends?
10 will you be rich/happy/hardworking?

This activity could be used with more advanced pupils to practise structures such as 'I'll probably be . . .', 'It's likely/unlikely that . . .'

WHAT WILL YOUR TOWN/YOUR HOUSE/YOUR SCHOOL BE LIKE IN 50 YEARS TIME?
This activity could be started as a series of questions to answer, with the option for more able pupils to add in their own detail later on.

You might use this activity to practise the same sort of vocabulary as the ideal house/town /school or you could use more vocabulary about the environment.

For example, will there be solar panels on your house/school?

IDEA
82

KEY ORGANIZATIONAL POINTS

1 Set a strict time structure for the production of this so that there is not too long a gap between pupils producing their articles and seeing the final version.

2 Do not be too ambitious to start with. A magazine consisting of one double-sided sheet of A4 that is finished is much better than a larger version which is never finished.

3 Remember that each different type of article could involve a lot of linguistic preparation so you could either limit your magazine to one or two types of writing or use the end of a term's work which has included writing the different types of article.

4 Linked to point 3 is the need for the magazine to be easily understood by the rest of the class.

CONTENT

1 Articles on famous celebrities. These can either be in note form or written out in sentences.

2 Articles on sports' results, fixtures. At its simplest this could be simply tables with headings such as 'Last Saturday's results', 'The draw for this season'.

3 Past-tense accounts of school trips, in which a number of pupils in the class would have participated.

4 Wordsearches, simple crosswords, picture crosswords, anagrams.

5 An interview with . . . (headteacher/foreign language assistant/visitor). Make sure the interviewee is appropriately linguistically briefed beforehand and sees a copy of the final article before you print it.

6 Adverts or special offers.

7 Lonely hearts column.

8 Horoscopes.

9 Problem page (difficult language).

10 News items – either about something happening in the school or outside. (There is a real problem with the news becoming quickly out-of-date, so pick your items carefully.)

Instead of a magazine, you can simply produce a puzzle sheet – all pupils make up a puzzle and you duplicate the best as a sheet for the whole class to do.

Before embarking on any of these activities, it can be well worthwhile talking to colleagues who teach pupils drama in their mother tongue to find out what sort of things pupils do, if they evaluate their own work and that of other pupils and what criteria they use.

Topics which lend themselves well to pupils performing dialogues or conversations include:

1 Café/restaurant scenes – food, opinions, complaints.
2 Shopping scenes – food, clothes, complaints.
3 Hotel, campsite, youth hostel – booking, complaints.
4 Bag snatching.
5 Hijacking, kidnapping.
6 Road accident.

GROUP SIZE

A group of more than four usually becomes unmanageable and tends to leave some pupils with little to do, so organize groups of two, three or four. Insist that everyone must have a part.

WRITING THE SCRIPT

Give pupils a definite time limit and clear instructions about what the scene is to be about. Insist that all members of the group write out all parts of the script so that they are all involved in writing it, no matter how big or small their individual part is. This stops a lazy pupil from simply writing out his/her own tiny part. Remind pupils that you will be taking in their books and giving marks for their script. Make sure that they have access to appropriate vocabulary lists. Encourage pupils to keep more or less to the language that you have been practising as otherwise it becomes very difficult for the rest of the class to follow and they are likely to lose interest.

ACTING

This activity follows on from the previous one.

BRINGING IN PROPS

If pupils write their script one lesson and then act out their scenes in the next lesson, this will enable them to bring in props for the actual performance. A gap between the writing and the performance will also allow you to take in their books and correct them. Allow pupils some time at the beginning of the next lesson to rehearse their script again. Whether you allow them to read from their books or learn their part off by heart will depend on how much time you have to spend on the activity.

ENCOURAGING PARTICIPATION

Make sure pupils know you expect them all to participate. You can make the activity part of a speaking assessment, if you feel that pupils are not taking it seriously. Show that you will not tolerate any rudeness from the audience.

USING THE VIDEO CAMERA

You can use a video camera to record the final version and this can help to motivate pupils to perform as well as possible, although it may inhibit some pupils so you will have to use your judgement. However, do not tie yourself up with the videoing as you need to be in control of the class. Use a pupil instead. It helps if you are able to borrow small clip-on microphones for your performers so that they can be heard easily. Encourage your camera operator to try and focus the camera on the whole group and not to move around or you will all feel rather seasick when you watch it.

EVALUATION

You can run the activity as a competition with marks for each group. The judge could be another teacher or pupils can judge. To organize pupil judging, decide what the scoring system is, out of three or out of five. Then ask all pupils who would give one point to raise their hands, then two, etc. and add up the score. You could give one score for words and one for acting skills/costume.

Pupils prepare a fashion parade with a commentary. You will need one lesson in which they prepare the work and then a second lesson when they bring in the clothes they want to wear in the fashion parade. If it goes well you may wish to repeat the parade for a parallel class or for a VIP, such as a senior member of staff. With additional practice, this can be a good item to present to a wider audience such as parents or parents of prospective pupils to the school, as everyone can enjoy the visual aspect of the activity even if they do not understand the language.

PREPARATION

Pupils will need access to appropriate vocabulary, such as describing the models: 'Here we have . . . wearing . . .', and a wider range of vocabulary for clothes and accessories than the average textbook will have. Access to a native speaker or a clothing catalogue can be useful here.

LESSON 1

Pupils work in groups of two, three or four. They need to decide who will be the model or models and what clothes they are going to wear. They must then write the commentary, decide who is going to narrate which bit and practise their script. Insist that everyone in the group must participate, either as a model or as a narrator. Try to get round the groups effectively to check their scripts. Make sure they write a list of who is bringing what for next lesson. As well as clothes, they may wish to bring in some suitable music.

LESSON 2

Decide on a venue for this lesson. You may be able to use a drama room. Otherwise clear appropriate space in the classroom. Allow pupils some organizational time at the beginning of the lesson to get changed and practise their script. Then do the fashion parade. To avoid argument, you can number the groups and pull numbers out of a hat to decide the order they go in. Insist on good behaviour from the audience. You can run it as a competition with marks for each group. The judge could be another teacher or pupils can judge. To organize pupil judging, decide what the scoring system is, out of three or out of five. Then ask all pupils who would give one point to raise their hands, then two, etc. and add up the score.

Using ICT

Computers are very useful for helping all pupils to produce professional-looking display work, no matter what their artistic talent or their handwriting ability.

Topics can include leisure centre posters, tourist information, hotel details, fashion parade, ideal uniform, ideal home, weather forecasts, healthy eating or any other topic for which informative posters or illustrations are appropriate.

PREPARATION

Make sure that you are familiar with and can explain to pupils how to do the following:

1 how to access the word-processing program(s) that your pupils will be using;
2 how pupils should save their work;
3 how to write text including any accents you need;
4 how to change the font, script and colour if a colour printer is available;
5 how to insert a picture or graphics;
6 what the print arrangements are. Is it black and white or colour? Make it clear to pupils if you want to check their work before they print to avoid waste.

Decide where pupils are going to find appropriate pictures or materials; your IT colleagues will know what picture banks are on your computers. Decide if pupils are going to have direct access to the internet or if you will need to access the internet yourself and download and paste materials into a folder for them. Details about hotels, tourist and leisure facilities in the target language are usually plentiful, but if pupils are accessing them for themselves you will need sites you can suggest or they may waste a lot of time. Bilingual sites are useful as pupils can work out what things mean for themselves.

Give pupils clear instructions about what to produce, or show them an example. Make sure they have access to the language they will need. Give them a time limit.

We often think of preparing PowerPoint presentations as something that the teacher does, but, in fact, asking pupils to prepare PowerPoint presentations is a good way of motivating pupils to consolidate vocabulary, especially if you allow them to include a few special effects.

TOPICS

Any topic which lends itself to visual presentation can be revised this way. A simple example is asking pupils to make slides which each consist of one weather picture and the appropriate weather phrase. A more complicated task is an account of a holiday in the past or an ideal holiday with pictures such as a means of transport, a hotel, a beach, etc., and pupils type in sentences to tell the story. You can ask different pupils to work on different topics which means that when you watch the slide shows as a class you revise more topics and, of course, you can add them to your departmental resource bank!

PREPARATION

Make sure you know how to type text into PowerPoint including accents if needed, insert pictures and press the special effects buttons. Decide where pupils are going to find appropriate pictures; your IT colleagues will know what picture banks are on your computers or may suggest internet sites.

Give pupils clear instructions and a realistic time limit. Allow time at the end of the lesson or in a future lesson to view the results.

Extrovert pupils have always enjoyed playing teacher and coming out to the board or making transparencies for the OHP, but with PowerPoint you can encourage shyer pupils to allow the class to see their work as no one actually has to stand in front of the class if they do not want to.

USING A DIGITAL CAMERA

You or the pupils can take pictures and incorporate them into written work on the computer.

TOPICS

Could include:

o pictures of themselves* to accompany descriptions or introductory letters;
o pictures taken around the school – outside, inside, headteacher, etc., to accompany a description of their school;
o pictures pupils have taken outside school that they bring in on disk or they email to school.

PREPARATION

Be sure to sort out the technical issues before embarking on this activity with a class. Currently the simplest system is probably to use a digital camera. Show the pupils how to take and how to load pictures onto the computer. Make sure they know how to save their work. You may also decide to show them how to move and edit a picture.

If you have never done this before, try the following: equip pupils with appropriate vocabulary for them to be able to write an introductory letter about themselves. As soon they get started, very quickly, go around the class taking a portrait picture of each pupil. You can then give the camera to one of the pupils who loads their photo onto their computer and then passes it on to the next pupil for them to do the same.

* If you are using pictures of pupils, check if there is a list confirming which parents allow you to photograph pupils. Have an alternative ready for those pupils you cannot photograph, such as a picture of the school badge.

Language teachers have often encouraged pupils to write and carry out surveys in order to practise the skills of asking as well as answering questions. This can be made more meaningful by helping pupils to convert their results into computer graphics such as pie charts or bar charts, labelled in the target language, which can be displayed on the wall.

PREPARATION
Make sure you are familiar with the programs that you are going to use, how the information is fed in and how it is represented. Find out what experience your pupils have had of these programs.

TOPICS
Topics which can lend themselves to survey questions include: asking pupils about their favourite TV programmes, music, bands, school subjects, football teams, how many brothers and sisters they have, which area of town they live in, aspects of daily routine, such as what they had for breakfast, what time they get up, etc.

If you are going to use computer graphics to represent the findings of your survey, you will need to anticipate the types of answers that you will get and how these can be represented visually.

1 You can ask closed questions which will produce a yes/no answer which you can then represent as a pie chart or bar chart.
2 You can use questions in which you give the respondent a limited number of options to choose from.
3 You can give respondents open-ended questions where you anticipate that you will get a fair number of similar responses and then you can create a category of 'other'.

Give pupils clear guidance and help in writing the questions. For pupils with limited linguistic skills, you may provide a list of questions from which they choose a few, or you may provide model questions which they can adapt by changing one word (for example what is your favourite . . .).

USING ICT TO PRODUCE SURVEYS

Tell pupils how many questions to write and how many people to interview and show pupils how to use the computer program to illustrate their results. You may prefer to do the survey one lesson and the IT work the next.

Email has made the whole idea of penfriends much more interesting and up-to-date. In the past, the time lag between pupils writing letters and receiving replies led to a loss of momentum and interest. Now that we have the technological means to overcome this, we need to make sure that we do not spoil this activity through bad planning.

Organize this activity as a class-to-class exchange rather than just individual pupils corresponding. Within the class, pair up pupils, but all the pupils in the class can access all the email letters, which makes it easier to share when the numbers are uneven or individual pupils are away and do not write a letter.

Do not be too ambitious about how much you put in each email. It is more motivating for pupils to have a more frequent exchange of emails than to take so long writing the first one that it uses up all the pupils' linguistic resources and may never get sent.

TECHNICAL DETAILS

First find out how pupils will be able to use email. It may be that they will have to send you their letters on an internal intranet system and then you can forward them to the foreign school. Draw up a precise timetable with your foreign school, including dates and topics. Book the IT facilities well ahead in your own institution. Your plan could look something like the following. This would give you a week to check up that the reply emails had arrived and do any linguistic preparation needed before reading them with pupils.

Tues, 1 October	School A – pupils write and send introductory emails with their name, age, brothers & sisters, pets.
Wed, 9 October	School B pupils read school A's introductory emails and send similar emails back.
Tues, 15 October	School A pupils read school B's replies and send emails with a short description of themselves and a photo (see Idea 88 on using the digital camera).

Other topics could include:

1 where they live and a map showing these places
2 description of the school
3 hobbies
4 sport
5 music/celebrity likes/dislikes
6 daily routine
7 the weekend – past, present or future

This is an extension of simple emailing that I have used for coursework with a class of 22 GCSE Italian pupils. The idea is equally valid as an exercise for pupils, who are not doing this form of coursework, to help any pupils who want to carry out a survey.

It was particularly useful for us because the Italian postal system at that time was not speedy and we needed replies by a certain date in order for pupils to finish their coursework, and we did not want a situation in which a pupil did not receive a reply. The theme for the coursework was to compare aspects of Italian life with aspects of British life.

1 Pupils wrote a letter asking questions about certain aspects of Italian life (food, daily routine, school, etc.). Pupils included items that were of particular interest to them, such as what type of mobile phone covers the Italians had. The handwritten copy of their initial letter was kept as part of their coursework, but they typed it into the computer and emailed it to Italy.

2 The Italian pupils then sent their replies.

3 Our pupils then wrote up a comparison between the Italian way of life and the British way of life. They were using genuine source material sent by Italian pupils but having to change around the I/we statements to they/the Italians. This comparison was then submitted together with their initial letter as their coursework.

4 In cases where pupils did not feel that they had written enough, they could email more questions to Italy and obtain more replies to help them extend their work.

EMAIL AS COURSEWORK

Divide the class into pairs/teams. Start with everyone typing a news story. Every few minutes signal that more details have surfaced about the story and that one pupil from each team has to come out to collect a strip of paper with the additional information to be incorporated into the story. Information always comes in a little faster than pupils can cope with to add a sense of excitement. When time is called, the teams must print out their stories and the most complete one wins.

TOPICS

Any topic which uses vocabulary that pupils can cope with, for example an account of a discovery of a shipwreck (can find all sorts of things), a celebrity wedding (can say who is there, what they are wearing, etc.).

PREPARATION

Type out the complete story, starting a new line for each statement. Put into largish font (at least 20 point) so that several pupils can read it together. Leave a couple of line spaces between each sentence so that you will be able to cut the story into strips and have a strip which is comfortable to hold (minimum width about 2cm). Make as many copies as you will have pairs/teams, preferably on stiff paper. Cut into strips and put all the sentence number one strips into one envelope, all the twos into another, etc.

At its simplest level, pupils receive the statements as full grammatical sentences in chronological order and merely type up the details, copying word for word. A slightly more advanced version involves using complete sentences but giving them to the pupils in the wrong order and they have to arrange them in the correct order (easiest version uses times, more complicated version uses phrases such as after lunch, before half-time, after opening the new hospital, etc.). More advanced again, the information arrives in note form and pupils have to write their account in correct grammatical sentences.

You will need two mobile phones, but one only need be used to receive the call. You can liven up the presentation of new work or act out a listening exercise by using mobile phones to simulate a telephone conversation, rather than merely reading it out. You can do this simply as a demonstration if you have the opportunity to team teach with a colleague or a language assistant. Alternatively you can involve pupils, preferably in the role of the client or the part of the dialogue that they are likely to need to say in real life or in the examination situation.

Topics which can be enhanced in this way include:

○ phoning for a pizza or phoning for a Chinese takeaway;
○ booking a hotel, campsite;
○ arranging to meet a friend.

Although you may not consider it entirely relevant to your examination work, pupils are often very interested in learning some of the text-messaging abbreviations that are commonly used. You can show them some examples of messages and even ask them to make some up, using the abbreviations.

MOBILE PHONES

RADIO INTERVIEW

Instead of simply asking each other questions on a topic, pupils work in pairs to write the script for a radio interviewer and a celebrity (sports personality, soap opera character, someone in a reality show such as *Big Brother*).

The secret with this is to encourage pupils to use the language that you have prepared with them and not to make up complicated answers that no one in the class will understand.

Drill the language that you are intending to use very thoroughly with pupils. This activity can be used for a range of quite simple topics such as hobbies, sport, personal information, daily routine, likes/dislikes, what you did last weekend, talking about a holiday or a sporting event in the past tense or talking about future plans.

Then ask the pupils to work in pairs to write the interview, with both partners writing down both parts. Set a time limit. Any pupils who finish before the end of the time limit should practise their dialogue as pairs. You may prefer to take in pupils' work at this stage to correct it and do the recording next lesson.

After pupils have practised in pairs, they come out to the front where you have prepared a microphone and a tape recorder. The pupils introduce themselves and they perform their interview to the class and you record it. Make sure the pupils are well-positioned for the microphone. You may need to encourage pupils by insisting that everyone must take part as it is part of their speaking assessment or by making it into a competition.

You can then pick two or three of the best ones (this will depend not just on the language but also on the clarity of the recording) and use them as a listening exercise with a parallel class who are working on the same topic. Likewise your class can receive some back and you will find that they enjoy the listening both for meaning and to see if they can guess to whom the voices belong.

TV INTERVIEW

For this activity, follow the same instructions as for the radio interview. This activity does however lend itself not just to interviews but also to a whole range of other scenes which can be acted out such as those in cafés, shops, etc.

PREPARATION

Make sure that you know how to work the video camera and that you have a suitably positioned TV screen to play back the video to the class. Whereas you would probably only choose a few radio interviews to present to the class, you will find that they will want to see all the TV recording.

Follow the same guidelines about careful linguistic preparation, clear instructions about the length and content, and a time limit. Just as you might want to take in the scripts to correct them before they perform them next lesson, putting off the filming until next lesson also allows pupils to bring in appropriate props.

Again, exchanging a finished video with a parallel class can be good fun.

Extended project activities

FUN WITH RECIPES 1

Learners of all ages enjoy talking about food. Using recipes also provides an opportunity to introduce learners to dishes which are typical of the target language countries.

Choose or write a recipe to suit the age of the learners, their experience in the kitchen and their linguistic ability. For young learners, it might be enough to do something very simple such as 'unwrap the cake, place the cake on a plate, arrange the biscuits around the cake'. On the other hand, with an enthusiastic adult learners' class, you could tackle an elaborate recipe from an authentic cook book.

1. JUMBLED COMMANDS

Write the commands in a jumbled order and ask the class to write them out in the correct order. This can be done as a simple worksheet. Alternatively, you can write each command on a separate strip of card and ask pupils to work in pairs to lay out the cards in the correct order.

2. MATCH UP THE TWO HALVES OF THE SENTENCE

This can be done as a gap-filling exercise or as pairs of cards that pupils have to match up. Ask pupils to match up the verb with the rest of the sentence, for example:

... *the oil into a saucepan*

... *the onion and the garlic into small pieces*

... *the onion and the garlic in the oil*

... *the tin of tomatoes and add to the vegetables in the saucepan*

... *the chopped basil onto the sauce and stir it in*

Choose one the following words for each gap: Pour Fry Sprinkle Chop Open

ICULASS

FIRST WATCH A CELEBRITY CHEF

Record a cookery programme from the television. If you can find a suitable programme in the target language, you can use it as a listening comprehension exercise, with activities such as true/false, gap-filling or comprehension questions.

If you can only get a programme in the pupils' mother tongue, or you would prefer to use a celebrity chef whom pupils will recognize, then you can always turn the sound down. You could then prepare your own script in language that is at an appropriate level for your pupils and read this out as you show the programme. If you want something simple, you may prefer to record a cookery demonstration from a children's programme.

YOUR TURN TO BE A CELEBRITY CHEF

If you have appropriate facilities, you can be the celebrity chef yourself and demonstrate the recipe! Give instructions as you go along and make pupils repeat the instructions bit by bit until they can recite the whole recipe.

NOW WRITE YOUR OWN RECIPE

Provide pupils with the appropriate vocabulary to write their own recipes. Again, for younger learners you might want to restrict this to something simple such as choosing items to go in a salad or a fruit salad. This means that you could keep the vocabulary simple, just using verbs such as *wash, peel, chop, add* and *stir*, together with the vocabulary for appropriate ingredients.

For more advanced students, provide examples of authentic recipes as there are specific terms that are used in recipes.

NOW THEIR TURN TO BE A CELEBRITY CHEF

If you have appropriate facilities, when pupils have written their own recipes and you have checked their linguistic accuracy it may be possible to allow some of them to demonstrate their recipes to the rest of the class! Make sure that they say each instruction clearly and make the rest of the class repeat the instructions over and over again so that they are really learning the appropriate language.

FUN WITH RECIPES 2 – BE A CELEBRITY CHEF

SELL THAT PRODUCT

For this activity, focus on up-to-date technological products that will interest your students, such as the latest mobile phones, music players or digital cameras.

1   Introduce the basic vocabulary by using descriptions taken from catalogues.

2   Then practise the language needed to explain what the product can do by using phrases such as 'it can . . .' or 'you can . . .' For example, you can take photos, you can make video clips, you can download music from the internet, you can copy, you can store . . .

3   Provide practice of the question forms as well. This could be done as a guessing game in which you show pupils a number of items, for example computer, mobile phone and camera, and then you pick one but do not tell the pupils which one. Pupils then have to ask you questions until they can identify the one that you have chosen.

4   Further practice can be carried out by making up comprehension activities in which pupils match statements, fill gaps, etc.

5   Once pupils have practised all the necessary vocabulary thoroughly, they can choose a product and write a convincing sales pitch about it, saying all the things that it can do, for example, it can store . . ., it can send . . . They can then read their descriptions out to the class.

6   As an extension, pupils can act out the role of an enthusiastic salesperson, saying all the things that the device can do.

7   If the equipment is available, they can make a video clip in the style of a TV advert, saying what their chosen gadget can do.

1   Make sure that the pupils are thoroughly familiar with
    the necessary vocabulary, having worked through
    Idea 98. This might include verbs such as you
    can . . . , it can . . . , it has . . . , it weighs . . . , it
    costs . . . , it is available in . . . (three colours, two
    sizes, all branches of . . .).

2   Ask them to invent/design their own model. For this
    they can work in pairs, groups or as individuals. With
    less advanced learners, encourage them to re-use the
    vocabulary they have already practised with small
    modifications such as cost, colour, etc. More
    advanced learners can be more adventurous and
    creative about their product.

3   Add a competitive element. You can organize this
    activity as a competition, with pupils presenting their
    product to the class and the class voting on the best.
    You can ask them to mark each other's products using
    specific criteria, for example price or usefulness.

4   As a further extension, pupils can work as a sales
    team to produce
    ○ a written advertisement
    ○ a website advertisement
    ○ a catalogue entry
    ○ a script for a salesperson (they can make this
       into a video clip if time and facilities allow it)

5   Demanding customers: when one group is presenting
    their product to the class, you can prepare the class to
    act as demanding customers, asking questions about
    the product. These can be simple questions such as
    'Can you . . . ?' or more awkward questions.

DESIGN A PRODUCT

PROMOTE YOUR AREA/ PROMOTE A TOURIST RESORT

Pupils can work as individuals or in pairs or groups. Ask them to imagine that they have to market either their home area or a well-known place in the country of the target language. Practise the necessary language such as 'there is . . .', 'you can . . .' together with the appropriate vocabulary (sights, facilities, etc.).

Pupils can then be asked to provide promotional material in a number of different formats, thus re-using and practising the necessary language. If pupils are working in groups they could share out the tasks. You could ask pupils to write the necessary text in the following formats:

○ a written poster
○ a written brochure
○ a PowerPoint presentation
○ a website
○ a script of a spoken advert (e.g. a radio advert) which pupils can then record
○ a script for a visual presentation (to accompany PowerPoint images or video clips)

Brochures and websites can provide useful materials such as pictures, but teachers may prefer to produce their own example text as brochures can use very advanced language. For example, you might want to teach 'You can visit the castle' whereas a brochure might say 'Perched high on a sandstone outcrop . . .'

The more advanced pupil

This activity is designed to teach the language of prohibition, permission and obligation. Drill pupils thoroughly in the phrases they are likely to need to use, such as must, must not, can, cannot, will not, not allowed to, ought not have. Then give pupils their cue cards and ask them to prepare a conversation.

SNAKE ON THE BUS

SNAKE ON THE BUS

Card one

You are a passenger on a bus. You suddenly realize that the stripey scarf worn by the man next to you is a snake not a scarf! You scream!

Card two

You are a snake charmer and you always take your snake Sissie, who is quite harmless, everywhere with you. You have never seen a notice prohibiting snakes on buses.

Card three

You are driving your bus when suddenly a passenger screams that there is a snake on the bus. You think that you had better ask the snake charmer to get off the bus.

Card one

You are a visitor to a zoo and you complain to a zoo keeper that an elephant has eaten your glove. You cannot see any notice warning visitors that the elephant is a thief.

Card two

You are a zoo keeper who is tired of stupid visitors who feed the elephant and lose their gloves.

Card three

You are a visitor to a zoo who hears another visitor complaining to the zoo keeper about the elephant eating his/her glove. You listen to them arguing and then give your opinion.

OTHER SCENARIOS

Restaurant owner/smoker/other clients.
Art gallery attendant/tourist taking photo.
Church warden/tourist wearing shorts.

This activity is similar to the snake on the bus conversations but practises the language of pleading, convincing and making excuses. First practise the sorts of structures that pupils are likely to need, such as ways of saying sorry, you did not mean to, if only you understood the problems I've got, etc. Then give them the cue cards and ask them to prepare a conversation.

PARENT/TEENAGER ROW

Card one: You are a parent who is furious because your son/daughter has arrived home late and did not bother to phone you.

Card two: You are a teenager who has arrived home late because . . .

MOTORIST/TRAFFIC WARDEN

Card one: You are parked on a double yellow line . . . (because you are getting tablets for your mother who will die if she does not get them immediately).

Card two: You are a traffic warden who is tired of lazy motorists parking on double yellow lines.

OTHER SCENARIOS

Store detective/shoplifter.

Police officer/drug user.

Referee/footballer who is being sent off.

Train ticket inspector/passenger without a ticket.

Motorist who has just reversed into another motorist.

This activity is useful for practising the language needed for expressing opinions and the language related to a specific topic such as an environmental issue. Tell pupils that they will all be taking part in a local radio phone-in programme about a proposal which is causing controversy in the neighbourhood, for example a new incinerator plant by a school, new airport, a proposed nightclub or pleasure park near an old people's complex.

You can either give pupils a free choice about the views they wish to express or you can give them a specific role to play (for example young Sam in favour of . . ., old Professor Jones against . . .).

Make sure that pupils have practised the type of phrases that they will need, such as 'It is scandalous that . . .' Give them a set time or a homework in which to prepare their radio slot. Then the teacher or a confident pupil plays the radio presenter and orchestrates the debate, bringing in the various pupils to express their views.

RADIO PHONE-IN

It can sometimes be difficult to interest young people in current affairs and politics and so you can find yourself teaching the concepts as well as the target language. One way to combat this alienation is to personalize it. Sketch a desert island on the board, a ship sinking just off the island and a few pin people on the shore. Tell the class to imagine a small group of people (including the class) shipwrecked on a desert island. Discuss the issues listed below with pupils in the target language. If you still think that it will be difficult to get pupils to respond, then prepare a worksheet with questions and possible answers so that pupils only have to choose an answer. This will be useful for pupils when you ask them to do follow-up written work, describing how life is organized on the island.

o How do they make decisions? (unanimous/majority voting). If there are nine of us, can we all share the decision-making? What happens if there are 30 of us? Or 200 of us? Or the whole school? (politics)

o How old do you have to be to share the decision-making? (politics)

o What are our priorities? Finding food? Building a shelter?

o Do we all work? Is there an age when you are too young or too old to work? Do we all work for a set number of hours or until we have brought back a certain amount of food?

o How do we share out food? Look after the injured? What do we do about Jane whose leg was bitten off by a shark while swimming ashore and who cannot help look for food? Should we bring her food? Is there anything she could do so she does not feel she is a burden? (social welfare/dignity for the disabled/taxation)

o What rules do we live by? What do we tolerate? What do we punish? (murder? theft? rape?) How do we punish? Can we afford two people to guard one person when we need everyone to gather food? (law)

o Should we let John have a day off work so he can write a song and entertain us this evening? (How do societies pay for the arts?)

- What do we do about Ben who is lazy – always late starting work, full of excuses about being ill, stops working when he thinks no one is looking? (absenteeism, scroungers)
- Rachel says she can make a fishing rod and a little dug-out canoe and go and fish for us, but as this is risky because of the sharks, should she be rewarded for this? (pay differentials)
- Should anyone educate the children? What should they learn?
- Another ship is wrecked and we can see people swimming towards our island. Do we let them land? (asylum seekers and immigration)

As with the desert island scenario, this is a way of introducing and practising the language needed to discuss some of the difficult concepts of the world of work.

You tell a story based on a brief history of the Industrial Revolution and draw the parallels with workplace issues today. If you feel a bit uncertain about this, ask your history or economics colleagues for a quick lesson. But remember that you are only using this as a vehicle to practise the language pupils need to understand and talk about the world of work. You can liven it up with your own little sketches or pictures from history books or you can use current cartoon characters to run your factories. Again you may prefer to prepare a worksheet with questions and suggested answers to help pupils express themselves and use the new vocabulary.

o We set up a factory.
o A rival sets up a factory with better machinery producing goods more cheaply.
o What do we do? Cut wages? Sack workers? Invest in new machines? All work longer hours? Cut profits? Cut the boss's pay?
o Is there any benefit for the bosses in all agreeing to keep wages low?
o Do bosses like a situation of high unemployment because people will be willing to work for low wages?
o What can workers do to stop wages being driven down? Are workers better off if they all act together or if they all do their own thing?
o What are trade unions for?
o Cheap foreign imports flood the market (cf. IT work outsourced).
o What do we do? Trade barriers?

Nowadays you do not need to worry about bringing back newspapers from your holidays or going to the one shop in town which sells foreign papers as you can find up-to-date newspaper headlines on the internet.

1 Pupils match up headlines and pictures. This can involve either very different topics or similar topics.
2 Pupils match up headlines and articles.
3 Pupils have the headlines in front of them. You then read out the first few lines of an article and pupils have to decide which headline you are referring to.
4 Pupils are given a number of newspaper headlines and they have to say which one they would use as their main headline and why ('because it is scandalous'). You can discuss whether their main headline would vary according to what sort of newspaper it is (intellectual or popular) or whether it is a daily or a weekly or whether it is a local or a national paper.
5 Use headlines to analyse the type of language and abbreviations that they contain.
6 If your pupils have access to the internet, you can ask them to bring in yesterday's headlines and explain in a couple of sentences what they are about.

Write a series of questions which you can ask pupils about an advert. Make them answer the questions in full sentences so that they have the opportunity to practise the language needed to describe an advertisement. Then, for further practice, ask the pupils the same questions about other advertisements. You can use either newspaper adverts or TV adverts that you have recorded from satellite TV. The questions could include the following:

1 Is it amusing or boring?
2 Is it informative?
3 Is it truthful or is it deceitful?
4 Does it describe the product?
5 Does it make you want to buy the product? How? Why?
6 Who is it aimed at? (adults/children/men/women)
7 Does it use animals/cartoons/children?
8 Does it exploit women?
9 Does it have a double meaning? Pupils may need some help in answering this question about a foreign advert.

Then you can ask pupils to write up their observations about one or more of the advertisements as a paragraph. Once pupils have written about specific advertisements, it becomes easier to discuss advertising in general.

As pupils become more advanced, they will be expected
to understand a wider range of newspaper and magazine
articles and be up-to-date with current affairs. Some
articles in textbooks can date very quickly and teachers
are left finding their own more recent articles and having
to think of ways of exploiting them. These are some of
the question techniques that are used by exam boards:

1   True/false (and correct the false sentences)
2   True/false/can't tell
3   Gap-filling with
   a) the exact number of words needed provided;
   b) with the correct words and distractors provided;
   c) with no words provided
4   Multiple-choice questions
5   A table to fill in with details from the text
6   Matching beginnings and ends of sentences with the
   exact number of sentences or with distractors
7   Questions in the mother tongue
8   Questions in the target language
9   Writing a summary of the news item or article in the
   target language or in their mother tongue
10 Translation of extracts from the article into the
   pupils' mother tongue
11 What these numbers refer to
12 Who these names refer to
13 Who these statements refer to
14 Finish the end of the sentence in your own words in
   the target language
15 Explain the meaning of these phrases in your own
   words in the target language

Other exercises can include:

16 Rewriting the article in a different tense (the article
   is about something that is going to happen and then
   pupils write about it as if it has happened)
17 Rewriting as full sentences information which has
   been given in note form, such as a portrait of a star
   giving details such as age and place of birth
18 Match a theme/word/sentence to a paragraph of the
   text

GETTING THE MOST OUT OF NEWSPAPERS

135

19 Find a word in the text with the same meaning/the opposite meaning
20 Retranslation back into the target language of some sentences that use the same vocabulary as the original passage

With the increased availability of satellite TV, it has become easier to obtain suitable materials, but it is not always easy to find appropriate programmes. The news is not always the best source as it tends to be read very fast for learners and it can be disheartening to spend a long time writing exercises about an extract, only for it to date very quickly. Often it is discussions, short extracts from speeches or documentaries which are easier for foreigners to follow and which may focus on issues that are likely to remain current for some time.

In addition to the range of question types suggested for reading comprehension on the previous page, TV recordings can also be exploited in the following ways.

1 Exercises that require pupils to listen very carefully to sections of the text and transcribe words or phrases
   a) to put into a gap-filling exercise;
   b) to complete a sentence;
   c) to answer target language questions.
2 Exercises involving writing down numbers, percentages or dates as pupils often find these very difficult.
3 Writing down an email address or a website reference.
4 Some questions to elicit comments from pupils about what they can see as well as what they can hear.

SATELLITE TV

Although pupils nowadays are familiar with the internet, they often have difficulty in finding things in the target language. Some exam options require project work, coursework or prepared topics for oral exams.

1   Make sure that pupils have good access to the internet.
2   Advise them on using appropriate search engines.
3   For their searches, advise them to use words or phrases that are not the same as the English and that are likely to be unique to the target language so that they do not have to waste time with a lot of English articles. If necessary suggest the words which they could put into their search.
4   With languages such as Spanish which are widely spoken, if they want to find out about Spain, it is very important to type in *en España* with the topic heading as otherwise they will also call up lots of material from South America and they may not realize that the information they get is not from Spain.
5   Skimming texts to see if they are relevant is a very difficult task for many pupils. You can suggest that they try to find some bilingual or multilingual sites such as the European Union which has versions of materials in all the official EU languages.
6   Find out if, in the target language, there are any children's websites that offer any simplified material.

Involving native speakers

The ideal for any language teacher is to facilitate contact between language learners and native speakers. This has a tremendous motivational effect as the learners begin to believe that the language they are learning is a reality. Furthermore, there are the obvious benefits of practising the language and having a genuine reason to use the language.

EXCHANGE VISITS

If it is possible to set up an exchange visit with a foreign school, then this offers a wealth of opportunity for using the language. However these opportunities need to be created as pupils on exchange visits often have difficulty finding things to talk about and there can be a tendency for them to stay within their own language group. It is important therefore to create situations in which the pupils work in mixed nationality groups and have to collaborate and communicate with the other members of the group in order to accomplish the task. This final section of this book suggests a few ways in which you can do that and have fun at the same time.

Do not forget to use your visitors not just with their hosts' classes but also with other classes in the school, and particularly with pupils who may have little opportunity to go abroad.

OTHER WAYS OF FINDING NATIVE SPEAKERS

As well as the obvious use of your foreign-language assistant or pupils who are visiting your school as part of an exchange or Comenius project, you can look for native speakers who are studying at your local university or groups of teenagers who have come to study in language schools. Organizers of such schools often welcome the opportunity for their pupils to undertake structured activities with other pupils.

If you cannot manage to get any native speakers into the school, then it is well worth establishing contacts with schools with whom you can exchange emails (see Idea 90 in Section 7).

Using native speakers offers unparalleled opportunities for pupils to use language for a genuine purpose, particularly if the native speaker is also sympathetic and can help the pupils with their language difficulties. As with any other activity, careful preparation is essential.

Ideally, you need about one native speaker of the target language to each group of four to five learners. If this is not possible, you could rotate with other activities in a carousel so that each group gets a turn with the native speaker.

Preparation: in the lesson(s) before the native-speaker visit give pupils opportunities to practise asking questions, as, so often, they are conditioned only to answer. You can encourage some creativity by asking them to suggest things that they would like to ask the native speaker. At the simplest level, they can ask 'Do you like . . .', including names of bands or football teams. You may like them to write down the questions in advance ready to do the interview.

For the lesson with the native speaker(s), arrange the pupils in groups of four or five. After 10–15 minutes, swap native speaker with another group. At the end, ask the pupils to feed back to you and the class what they have found out about their guest.

This is an extension of the interview idea, but all pupils can be involved both in writing the surveys and responding to the surveys. This can work well as a follow-up activity to the interviews with pupils, practising the same sort of language as they prepared for the interviews.

The organizational details will depend on the number and proportion of native speakers you have. Decide if all pupils should use one language or if pupils should write the questions in the language they are learning.

Provide plenty of linguistic support to help pupils write the questions and give clear instructions about how many questions they should write and how many people they should interview. Encourage pupils to write down their answers before they start circulating and to record the answers they receive.

See Idea 89 for further advice on question writing and on how the survey work could be followed up with display work that pupils label in both languages.

Safety first: check up on your school's guidelines for this type of activity. Make it quite clear to pupils that they must stay together within a designated area, preferably within your sight. When going outside the school grounds, make sure that you have the necessary permission from the home pupils as well as the foreign visitors. The entrance to a large supermarket can be a good place for this activity, often covered by security cameras, but have the courtesy to contact the store manager first. Make sure you have adequate staffing. You will need to use several venues if you have a large group of pupils. Alternatively, if the venue is very near the school, you can take one group out after another.

This activity may provide more linguistic opportunity for your foreign visitors than for the home pupils, but your pupils may be able to do something similar if they go abroad.

Organize the pupils to work in pairs to write three simple questions.

This activity can work well if the home pupil stops the passer-by, the foreign pupil asks the questions and the home pupil records the answers as the foreign pupil may have difficulty in understanding the passer-by's response, particularly if they have a strong regional accent, for example:

Home pupil: Good morning. Please could my French friend ask you three quick questions?
Foreign pupil: How often do you come to this supermarket?

See Idea 89 for further advice on question writing and on how the survey work could be followed up with display work that pupils label in both languages.

'Bring me' is a simple classroom game which starts with an easy command such as 'Bring me a book' and can progress to more demanding tasks such as 'a French pupil wearing an English school tie' or a 'French and a British pupil tied together'.

Divide the class up into mixed-language teams and make sure that you position yourself and the teams in such a way that the teams are equally distant from you and so that a representative of each team can come out to you without falling over the furniture.

You can shout out the command and then representatives from the team must bring out the item to you. You can award one point for every team that brings the item and two points for the team that brings it first. If you want to ensure that everyone in the team participates, you can number the pupils in each team (1, 2, 3, 4) and then say 'Bring me a pen, number 2'.

Alternatively, you can have each command written on a piece of card, with one card for each question for each team. Keep all the no. 1 questions in one envelope, all the no. 2s in another, etc. You can use a different colour for each team.

TREASURE HUNT

A treasure hunt can involve just the classroom or a larger area. Try to write the clues so that pupils will have to collaborate. For example, you can write the clues in the foreign language so that the guest pupils will understand them easily but they will have to communicate with the home pupils in order to find the places.

Give the pupils strict instructions about staying together and a return time.

Put pupils into mixed-language groups and give them some written instructions to follow to make something. At its simplest this can be a plan of a town, a school or a house which they have to draw following the instructions.

You can provide some instructions only in one language and some instructions only in the other language so that pupils can only complete the task if they have understood the instructions in both languages. Make each instruction short and clear, but warn pupils that they may need to read all the instructions before they begin.

For example, if doing a town plan, instructions can be 'Put the castle south of the river', 'Put the supermarket next to the castle', so they will need to experiment with a rough plan before they produce their final version.

If you can arrange access to suitable facilities and bring in the ingredients, pupils could follow instructions to make a typical dish. This activity can be particularly exciting for pupils who come from a country where food technology does not form part of the curriculum.

Other ideas that rely on understanding instructions include paper-folding activities such as making a paper hat or a paper boat. Pupils can then decorate the hats for a silly hats parade.

MAKE A CAKE, A HAT OR A TOWN PLAN

IDEA

117

MAKING A WALL MURAL
FOR THE CLASSROOM

The idea of this activity is that pupils have to communicate together in groups to produce a picture. You can choose a specific theme such as 'memories of our exchange visit' or 'international friendship'. The easiest way to organize this activity is to divide the pupils up into mixed-nationality teams and give each team a large sheet of paper on which to produce their final picture. You can then display the pictures in your own classroom or elsewhere as appropriate.

Give clear instructions about the theme and style of picture you want (for example writing/no writing). It might also be useful for pupils to have some rough paper on which to sketch out their ideas to start with. Pupils will also need appropriate drawing materials such as crayons, pens or paints.

If you are feeling more ambitious, you can use a wall of your classroom to produce a frieze. Cover the appropriate section of wall with paper and divide it up into sections for each team of pupils to work on. Towards the end of an exchange visit, you could make a visual diary with one section of the wall representing each day of the stay (for example 'Monday', 'Tuesday'). Make sure that there is enough room for pupils to work if they will be drawing directly onto the wall. Otherwise, use sheets of paper which you then pin up onto the wall.

CHALK OR PAINT A WALL OR CAR PARK

For the more ambitious, you can find a wall outside the classroom or you can give each team a parking space in a car park on which they draw a picture. This may sound far-fetched but it has been done (I have the video to prove it!). Each group of mixed-nationality pupils is given one space that they have to design and paint (can be permanent or can be chalk). Make sure you seek the appropriate permission beforehand!

You may be able to get advice or help from your art department or community artists. Have a camera ready to record your pupils' achievements, particularly if you use chalk in a rainy climate!

146

Pupils can work together in mixed-nationality teams to produce a model such as a castle. You can be very prescriptive by giving each team an identical set of materials and a precise task, such as 'Make a model of a medieval castle'.

Alternatively you can give a precise theme for the outcome but allow pupils a choice of materials. Or you can encourage creativity and suggest that pupils make their own sculpture using materials of their choosing.

Recycling and respecting the environment are often themes that schools choose to encourage. Your art department may help you find pictures of professional sculptures that have been made using recycled materials or you may know of some in your locality.

Materials can include old cardboard boxes, magazines, cans, used matchsticks, packaging, etc. You will need to encourage pupils and friends to help you build up a suitable collection of materials in advance. You will also need appropriate glue, sticky tape and string.

Give pupils clear instructions and a time limit.

WRITING EVALUATIVE COMMENTS IN THE TARGET LANGUAGE

Allow time at the end for pupils to view each other's work. You can also ask pupils to write a comment in both languages about each of the items seen. Make sure pupils have appropriate sentence models and vocabulary such as 'I like the statue of the dog because it is unusual'.

MAKING SCULPTURES

A 6-PHOTO DISPLAY

Ask pupils to select six photos to make a display to commemorate a visit.

You can limit it to a couple of hours' activity and just to what pupils can find in school or you can encourage pupils to take photos on their various activities throughout their stay. We used to have to dash down to the one-hour development service for this activity, but now with digital cameras and mobile phones, the possibilities are endless providing you know how to deal with the technology. Read Idea 88 on digital cameras and Idea 87 on PowerPoint displays in Section 7 for advice.

For this activity, pupils work in mixed-language teams and they must select just six photos to display. Alternatively, this can be a nice activity for your foreign pupils to carry out on their own with their own teachers at a time when perhaps the home pupils are busy with lessons. Make sure that they have the necessary technical support such as a technician or senior pupil.

They should write a caption or description for each in both languages, and should be able to justify their choice, for example 'I wanted to include a picture of the swimming pool because we do not have one in our school'.

A POWERPOINT PRESENTATION

Pupils work together in mixed-language groups to make a PowerPoint presentation incorporating some of the photos they have taken and a bilingual text.

Pupils really enjoy doing this and when the presentations are ready, you can invite senior staff to a presentation to add status to the event.

FOREIGN CORRESPONDENTS

You can imagine that the pupils who are here on a visit are foreign correspondents who are sending back a report each day to 'Head Office', namely the pupils they have left behind. Pupils can work collaboratively to prepare an email each day with the home pupil helping to facilitate the technical side of how to log on, how to include pictures, while the foreign pupil types in the message.

MUSIC

Pupils work together to compose a tune or an accompaniment together. Alternatively they can write and perform a song.

DANCE

Pupils can work together to produce a dance routine.

PUB-STYLE QUIZ

Pupils work in teams of four, either to answer a written set of questions or to respond to questions that are read out, with one short round in one language and one short round in the other language. Most of the questions should be realistically answerable by both nationalities with the occasional question where they are likely to have to rely solely on the pupils of one nationality.

OTHER ACTIVITIES

Mixed-language groups can also benefit from many of the activities mentioned elsewhere in this book, particularly the IT activities (Section 7) and the creative writing and acting out activities (Section 6).

MORE IDEAS FOR WORKING WITH NATIVE SPEAKERS

APPENDIX

1   Never use an overhead projector (OHP) without checking it and the transparencies beforehand. Check it is the correct distance away from the screen – the further away the bigger the image.

2   Check you can focus it, dust it, change a bulb and keep a spare bulb handy.

3   Make sure everything you prepare is legible from the back row – you will need to check with your OHP as it is positioned in your classroom – but as a general rule you will need a type size of about 24 point if you word-process your OHTs. You may find a font like Arial gives you the best clarity. Make sure you enlarge any printed images as necessary, before copying them onto OHT.

4   If photocopying onto to OHT, make sure you have the correct type of OHT for photocopying as other types may melt in the copier and cause very expensive damage.

5   Printer OHTs – you can get special OHTs for use with computer printers which can be useful if you want to produce colour OHTs, but they can be costly on ink. For black and white it is just as easy to print on paper and then photocopy.

6   If writing/drawing your own, use different colour pens to highlight grammatical points such as verb endings or simply for interest. Check colour visibility as strong sunshine makes some light colours very difficult to see and the light in the classroom may vary considerably at different times of day and in different weather.

REWARD SYSTEMS

Many schools now operate reward systems to motivate
pupils. If this is the case in your school, it is best to try to
link in any system you use in the languages department to
the overall school system. Rewarding pupils for oral work
is important in languages to encourage participation and
make them realize that speaking and listening work is as
important as written work. As a lot of language-learning
activities lend themselves readily to scoring and pupils are
motivated by frequent rewards, you may find that you
need a sub-unit of the school unit. For example, if the
school policy is to award a merit mark for an exceptional
piece of work, then you may decide that pupils need to
earn 3 or 5 points to gain a merit mark.

Points Chart

Pupils like to see their progress, so you can make a chart
on which you write a list of pupils' names in alphabetical
order and write up their points. Pupils seem to enjoy the
competitive nature of this. It is a good idea to appoint
a reliable pupil at the beginning of the lesson to write in
the points so that you simply have to say 'A point each
for John Jones and Jane Smith' and do not slow down
the pace of the lesson while you find the names yourself.
Make sure that unscrupulous pupils cannot add points
to the chart without you seeing, so either take the chart
away with you and only display it in the lesson, or make
sure that pupils are not in the room without you. You can
make it on OHT acetate and just display it to pupils at
the end of each lesson/week.